FORGOTTEN MIGRANTS

FORGOTTEN MIGRANTS

*Foreign Workers in Switzerland
before World War I*

Madelyn Holmes

Rutherford ● Madison ● Teaneck
Fairleigh Dickinson University Press
London and Toronto: Associated University Presses

Associated University Presses
440 Forsgate Drive
Cranbury, NJ 08512

Associated University Presses
25 Sicilian Avenue
London WC1A 2QH, England

Associated University Presses
P.O. Box 488, Port Credit
Mississauga, Ontario
Canada L5G 4M2

The paper used in this publication meets the requirements
of the American National Standard for Permanence of Paper
for Printed Library Materials Z39.48-1984.

Library of Congress Cataloging-in-Publication Data

Holmes, Madelyn, 1945–
  Forgotten migrants.

  Bibliography: p.
  Includes index.
  1. Alien labor—Switzerland—History.   2. Engineering
—Switzerland—History.   3. Switzerland—Economic
conditions.   I. Title.
HD8608.5.A2H64   1988   331.6'2'09494   87-45559
ISBN 0-8386-3304-8 (alk. paper)

PRINTED IN THE UNITED STATES OF AMERICA

To my parents,
Barbara Berch Jamison
and the late Dr. S. E. Jamison

CONTENTS

PREFACE

The foreign worker problem in Western Europe was the social issue par excellence, cause célèbre of humanitarians, for many years in the 1960s and 1970s. The problem was analyzed by scholars in economics, sociology, and political science. Journalists wrote muckraking reports on housing conditions and discrimination. A film satirizing the situation, *Bread and Chocolate*, had international box office success.

When I arrived in Zurich in 1973 as the wife of an American foreign worker, I naturally started to try to understand Switzerland's number one social problem. However, I soon realized that foreign workers in Switzerland were not a wholly new phenomenon. During the quarter century before World War I (1888–1914), they were also prevalent. Since there had been a substantial proportion of foreign workers in Switzerland at an earlier period, I began to consider the present situation from an historical perspective. I wanted to know what foreign workers had done in Switzerland at the beginning of the twentieth century. I wanted to know whether they had been regarded as a problem. As I began to investigate the subject, I decided to examine the historical migration as an economic issue rather than a social one.

Since I was familiar with studies about migration to the United States and had read countless numbers of reports about the effects of immigration on the growth of the economy, I began to look at the Swiss economy in a similar light. "The forgotten migrants" came during the period of Swiss industrialization, and I therefore decided to see whether they had had an effect on Swiss industry. I selected one Swiss industry to analyze in detail, the engineering industry, because it was a major employer of foreign workers during both the early 1900s and in the 1970s.

I left Switzerland in 1977 but continued my interest in this subject while teaching history in England. I received a British Social Science Research Council grant in 1979 to study the importance of foreign workers in the Swiss machine industry, 1850–1978. During several trips to Switzerland, I was able to collect data on which this book is based. Professor Rudolf Braun of the University of Zurich and Dr. Christian Müller of the *Luzerner Neuste Nachrichten*, as well as my long-held friends

Werner and Prue Ballmer of Schöfflisdorf (canton Zurich), helped me invaluably during these visits.

This study was written at the University of East Anglia in Norwich, England, during the years 1979–83. I am grateful to the distinguished faculty of economic historians in the School of Economic and Social Studies who contributed however indirectly and perhaps unknowingly to my understanding of Swiss economic history. In particular, European economic historian Alice Teichova and British economic historian Jim Holderness spent countless hours helping me develop an idea into a full-fledged research project. I also benefited from discussion with my colleague, Jonathan Steinberg of Trinity Hall College, Cambridge University.

I am grateful, above all, for the support of my family. To my parents, Barbara Berch Jamison of Fuengirola, Spain, and the late Dr. Saunders Eliot Jamison; to my husband, Lewis; and to my daughter, Amy, I thank you.

FORGOTTEN MIGRANTS

INTRODUCTION

Contemporary population movements from southern to central and northern Europe have been important to the political, social, and economic history of Europe since the end of World War II. During the two decades between 1955 and 1975 in particular, foreign workers and their families comprised sizable and growing minorities in several countries in Western Europe.[1]

The contemporary migration of population within the continent of Europe has been invariably discussed as a postwar phenomenon. In West Germany foreign workers, who were known as *Gastarbeiter* until 1970, were viewed as a necessary element in the postwar "economic miracle." In France, in addition to North Africans, southern European foreign workers bolstered labor force numbers. In the smaller countries of Western Europe, such as Sweden, Belgium, Luxembourg, Austria, and Switzerland, foreign labor supplemented indigenous manpower, allowing these economies to be included in the ranks of the most highly industrialized nations of the world.

Seldom has the contemporary intra-European migration been viewed in historical perspective. However, as this book describes in the case of Switzerland, this is not the first period in history that has seen mass intra-European movements of population. During the quarter century preceding World War I, a population movement of comparable dimensions and with similar destinations occurred. Poles worked in mines in the Ruhr region of Germany; Czechs sewed clothes and cobbled shoes in Vienna; and Italians constructed bridges, tunnels, and roads in France and Switzerland.

This book does not pretend to accomplish the worthy task of comparing contemporary intra-European migration with the earlier pre–World War I migration. In point of fact, it may be premature for that type of analysis, for recent data may not yet be complete. Scholars do not now know how longlasting or how socially, politically, or economically significant contemporary migration may have been. Nonetheless, for the purpose of understanding the past, it may be useful to write a few preliminary words of comparison about the two periods of migration to Switzerland.

Each wave of migration continued for approximately twenty-five years: from 1888 to 1914 and from 1946 to 1973. The later, or contemporary migration to Switzerland began almost as soon as World War II ended. Even though Switzerland had not been a combatant in the war, the Swiss economy and population had been mobilized and lived through the war years in a state of constant preparedness. At the conclusion of the war, therefore, there was a heightened demand for goods and workers.

The Swiss government issued permits to foreign workers, beginning in 1946. During the year 1946–47, the number of foreign workers, originating almost exclusively from Italy, increased from 50,000 to 150,000.[2] Twenty-four years later, the number of foreign workers in Switzerland amounted to 657,030, and the total population of the country in 1970 was 17 percent foreign born.[3] At the outset, the contemporary wave of migration was considered to be temporary. The Swiss government gave work permits in particular to workers without families. Not until the late 1950s did Switzerland, which was now competing with other European countries for foreign manpower, allow families to settle.[4] This changed the character of the alien population and brought forth reactions from the Swiss population. In the 1960s, economists were debating the effects of foreign workers on the economy, and xenophobic tendencies were spreading among the Swiss population. By 1963, the Swiss government began to restrict the number of foreign workers. However, the number continued to increase until 1973 when the government reduced the number of work permits issued.

The earlier migration to Switzerland started with a small number of migrants in the 1880s and reached a peak in the years immediately before World War I.[5] In 1910, 14.7 percent of the total population of Switzerland and 16.7 percent of the total work force were foreign.[6] The proportion of foreigners in Switzerland far exceeded the proportion of foreigners in any other European country: In 1910, Belgium had a foreign-born population of 3.1 percent; France, of 2.7 percent; and Germany, of 1.7 percent.[7] Foreign workers came to Switzerland at this time mainly from southern Germany and northern Italy.

In the case of German migration, a close connection existed between the pattern of German overseas emigration, internal migration within Germany, and intra-European migration.[8] As Germans emigrated to North America, workers from German territories east of the Oder River were employed in industries and mines in the Ruhr region. Germans who migrated from east Prussia were replaced on the estates there by east European agricultural workers. At the same time that Germans emigrated overseas to North and South America and east Europeans migrated to work in German mines and agricultural estates, Germans were also part of an intra-European population movement to Switzerland. German technicians, scholars, and merchants had migrated to neighboring European countries throughout the nineteenth century, but "this immigration became more intense the more oversea migration decreased."[9] During the period from 1888 to 1914, the number of Germans residing in Switzerland increased sharply.[10] At the outbreak of World War I, German migration to Switzerland subsided and was never again as significant as during the prewar period.

Italian migration to Switzerland was also only one aspect of a global Italian migration pattern. Intra-European migration of Italians was well established long before mass overseas movements began. Italian colonies existed in England, Switzerland, Germany, Belgium, and especially in France in the midnineteenth century.[11] Between 1876 and the outbreak of World War I, however, there was a significant increase in the number of Italian emigrants both within Europe and to overseas destinations. Approximately half of the fourteen million Italians who emigrated moved within Europe, and half went overseas.[12] Within the European continent, Switzerland was the favored destination for the largest number of Italians during the first decade of the twentieth century.[13] By 1914, with the onset of war, thousands of Italians returned home, and by 1920, the Italian population in Switzerland had decreased substantially.[14]

Swiss scholars have tended to emphasize the basic differences between the two periods of mass migration.

> The problem of foreigners before World War I represented an entirely different situation from the situation today. . . . In respect to age, family, occupation, income, social and educational structure there were not as substantial differences with the Swiss population as is the case today.[15]

Even though there were many dissimilarities, in some respects, the migrations were similar. The types of work in which the foreigners were employed and the countries from which they originated did not change significantly from the earlier to later periods. For the purpose of comparison, data from the Swiss censuses of 1910 and 1970 will be used, since they represent peak census years for each migration stream.

The largest employer of foreign workers in Switzerland in both 1910 and 1970 was the construction industry.[16] Before World War I, foreigners built railroads, tunnels, housing, and factories. During the 1950s and 1960s, foreigners provided the manpower for constructing highways, apartment buildings, and shopping centers, as well as civil engineering projects. In addition to construction, in 1910 foreign workers were numerous in the fields of household service, textile manufacture, clothing production, commerce, and tourism. In 1970, foreign workers were prevalent in the engineering industry, metalworking, commerce, tourism, and clothing production.

Both population movements included a substantial proportion of males as well as females.[17] Females did not work on construction projects, but in 1910, they worked in domestic service, textile factories, clothing production, tourism, and commerce. In 1970, female occupations did not differ markedly from the earlier period. Women worked in clothing production, health care, tourism, engineering factories, and did cleaning.

During both periods, the majority of migrants came from Germany and Italy, countries that border Switzerland to the north and south. In 1970, 54 percent of all foreigners came from Italy, and 10.9 percent originated from Germany. During the earlier migration, the proportions from Germany and Italy were nearly equal—36.7 percent came from Italy, and 39.8 percent came from Germany. However, in 1970, 20 percent of the foreigners came from nonneighboring countries.[18]

There were also elements of similarity in reactions by the Swiss population to the two migrations. During both periods, the Swiss showed concern about the substantial proportion of foreigners living in Switzerland. In 1910, concern was expressed as a fear of foreign economic, political, and cultural domination. In 1970, concern was expressed about foreigners not fitting into Swiss society.

A Swiss scholar wrote in 1965 comparing the two migrations:

> Before World War I foreigners living in Switzerland belonged to social classes comparable to those of the native working population. Presently, however, the foreign segment of the working population . . . swells the lowest social and economic classes of the Swiss population.[19]

This book analyzes the economic roles performed by foreigners in the decades before 1914 and demonstrates that foreign workers "swelled the lowest social and economic classes" in Switzerland during both periods of mass migration. This book, however, is not a comparative study but an in-depth analysis of the earlier migration, the forgotten foreign workers. It addresses the following two questions: (1) Why did migration to Switzerland occur during the period from 1888 to 1914? (2) How did migration affect the Swiss economy? Although reference is made to the employment of foreigners in the primary and tertiary sectors of the

Swiss economy, the main emphasis nevertheless is on the impact of foreign workers on the growth of Swiss industry.

Two Swiss industries in particular are the focus of more detailed analysis, namely, the textile and engineering industries. Since these are contrasting industries, their manpower demands differed, thereby providing the researcher with two distinctly separate examples of the relationship of foreign workers to Swiss industry. In the case of the engineering industry, at that time a relatively new and capital-intensive industry, male workers, traditionally from southern Germany but increasingly from northern Italy, brought technical expertise, skilled and unskilled labor to Switzerland. In the case of the textile industry, an older labor-intensive industry, unskilled female workers, mainly from northern Italy but also from southern Germany, were attracted to the expanding factories.

The answer to the question of why foreigners migrated to Swiss industry will be sought at the aggregate level, examining the motivations of the migrant groups. Furthermore, the answer will be sought by examining the pace and progress of industrialization in Switzerland. In other words, the analysis will consider the push exerted by labor-exporting countries on the one hand and the pull exerted by the labor-importing country on the other hand.

Since migration to Switzerland was so heterogeneous, it is necessary to describe at least two different functions that foreign workers performed in Swiss industry. Two roles have been identified and used in the analysis: The first is applicable to Italian foreign workers, and the second is associated mainly with German foreign workers. However, neither role is exclusive to one ethnic group alone, since some Germans fit into the category describing the Italian experience and vice versa. These two roles are: (1) Foreign workers, attracted to Swiss industry, provided the labor force necessary for the introduction of mass production methods of manufacture; and (2) foreign workers, attracted to Swiss industry, provided one linkage in the interdependent industrial development of central European economic regions.

Source material for this study came mainly from official Swiss documents written during the early twentieth century. A variety of statistical, economic, and social reports provided the backbone of the study. In particular, the analysis was based on data from Swiss censuses, factory inspectors and employers associations reports, and information from Swiss trade unions and the Swiss government's customs department. Accounts by contemporaries, academic analyses, and archive materials from a number of Swiss manufacturing companies broadened the perspective, supplementing official data.

The book is divided into eight chapters, organized within the framework of a push and pull analysis. The first two chapters are introductory. Chapter 1 briefly describes the setting—the Swiss economy during the quarter-century preceding World War I. It also relates the research to other academic studies on immigration. Chapter 2 describes the people who participated in the population movement from an aggregate, statistical viewpoint. A demographic and geographic description is presented.

Chapter 3 examines the push factors that motivated the intra-European migration. It analyzes internal conditions in southern Germany and northern Italy that encouraged a portion of the populations to migrate to Switzerland.

Chapters 4–7 describe the pull or attractions of the Swiss economy. Chapter 4 defines two roles that foreign workers performed in Swiss manufacturing industries. Chapters 5 and 6 are case studies of two Swiss manufacturing industries, each an illustration of how the combination of push and pull factors supplied manpower for Swiss industry. Chapter 5, a case study of the textile industry, is an example of a traditional industry. Chapter 6, a case study of the engineering industry, is an example of a modern industry. Chapter 7 examines the roles played by foreigners in the nonmanufacturing sectors of the Swiss economy: in the primary sector, construction, and the services.

Chapter 8, the conclusion, summarizes the roles that foreigners performed in the Swiss economy between 1888 and 1914.

1

THE SETTING

Switzerland, 1888–1914

In order to analyze why foreigners came to Switzerland during this period, it is necessary to understand something of the country's economic geography and history. Since 1848, when the federal constitution was adopted, Switzerland has existed in the same shape, size, and form, with twenty-two cantons (states).[1]

These cantons have divided governmental functions with the federal government, which is located in the capital city, Bern. The federal government has been responsible for foreign relations and the operation of services that the cantons have shared, such as post, mint, telephone, and the armed forces. Individual cantons have been responsible for the administration of educational, welfare, and land use policies, and community authorities have governed local affairs.

Swiss geography provides a valuable key for understanding the country's economic history. In particular, four features have made its history distinctive: the central position of Switzerland in relation to the continent of Europe, a harsh terrain, a scarcity of natural resources, and a diverse population.

Switzerland's situation in Europe has made it a transit route for armies, commerce, and population since Roman times.[2] Although the country has no outlets to the sea and no important ports with the exception of Basel on the Rhine River, nevertheless it has been a center for foot, road, rail, and recently air transport. European trade from north to south and east to west has passed through Switzerland for centuries. During the second half of the nineteenth century, transport by rail was greatly expanded. By 1900, nearly four thousand kilometers of railway lines were in operation in Switzerland.[3] Gotthard Tunnel (1882), Simplon Tunnel (1906), and Lötschberg Tunnel (1913) provided rail links through the alps. Switzerland is also connected to several other countries in Europe through two major river systems. The sources of the Rhine and Rhone rivers are both found within the country; only the Rhine, how-

19

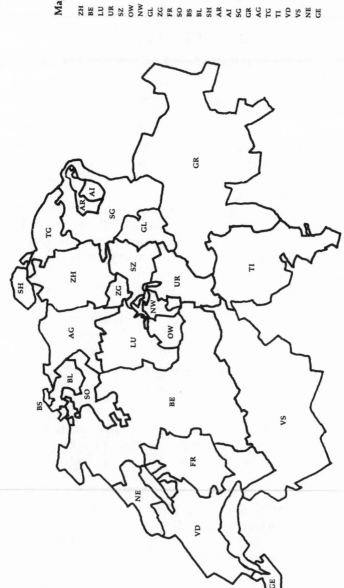

Map of Switzerland

ZH	Zurich
BE	Bern
LU	Lucerne
UR	Uri
SZ	Schwyz
OW	Obwalden
NW	Nidwalden
GL	Glarus
ZG	Zug
FR	Fribourg
SO	Solothurn
BS	Basel-Town
BL	Basel-Country
SH	Schaffhausen
AR	Appenzell Ausser Rhoden
AI	Appenzell Inner Rhoden
SG	St. Gall
GR	Grisons
AG	Aargau
TG	Thurgau
TI	Ticino
VD	Vaud
VS	Valais
NE	Neuchâtel
GE	Geneva

ever, has been used for transportation. In addition, four lakes of continental importance are partly located in Switzerland—Lake Geneva, Lake Constance, Lake Maggiore, and Lake Lugano.

Switzerland's harsh terrain has always made agriculture difficult: Only one-quarter of the land has the potential to produce crops.[4] Nonetheless, in 1875, Swiss farmers were still able to supply 70 percent of domestic grain requirements.[5] However, the agricultural crisis that affected all of Europe at the end of the nineteenth century transformed agricultural production in Switzerland. Countless Swiss farmers emigrated overseas, and the agricultural industry that remained relied primarily on livestock production. The number of cattle, for instance, increased from 900,000 in 1855 to 1.5 million by 1905, and the cheese export business expanded manifold during the period.[6] Animal production makes best use of the country's natural landscape, for the hilly and mountainous areas, although unsuitable for arable use, can be well used as pastures.

The harsh terrain has been responsible for the growth of another industry, namely, tourism. Since Albrecht von Haller in his poem "The Alps" (1732) and Jean Jacques Rousseau in his novel *La nouvelle Héloïse* (1756) pointed out the inherent beauty of mountain landscapes, the world's artists, poets, and adventurers have publicized the attractions of Switzerland's harsh terrain. During the nineteenth century, the well-to-do from England, the United States, and Europe started visiting Swiss mountain resorts, bringing about "a real flowering of the Swiss tourist industry around the turn of the century."[7]

In contrast to other industrializing economies of Western Europe, Switzerland lacked many of the natural resources necessary for the development of heavy industry. Coal reserves were insufficient even in the early nineteenth century when the level of industrial production was low. In recent decades, lack of oil has made it one of the most energy import-dependent nations in the world.[8] However, in the nineteenth century, Switzerland used the natural resources it did have: iron, wood, water power, salt, building materials, silk, and milk, and the origins of major Swiss industries can be traced back to the existence of these raw materials.

Switzerland never had extensive reserves of iron ore, but in the midnineteenth century when Swiss demand for iron was still limited, domestic reserves were able to supply 42 percent of Swiss demand.[9] In this century, the country has relied on less expensive iron imports except during the world wars when Swiss iron was in demand and was exported to Germany, Belgium, and Czechoslovakia.[10] With one-quarter of its land area covered by woodland, such Swiss industries as paper, construction, watches and clocks, toys and woodcrafts have used indigenous reserves of wood. Similarly, vast reserves of water power led to the early development of an electrical supply industry, production of aluminum, electrical engineering, and the electrification of the railways.

Switzerland has always had abundant raw materials for construction: stone, sand, marl, chalk, gravel, and gypsum.[11] They have been found mainly in the Jura mountains and prealpine regions. In addition granite, mostly from Uri and Ticino, and slate, mostly from Glarus, were native building materials widely used in the nineteenth century. Although Switzerland did not have "most of the raw materials such as coal, brimstone or pyrites, phosphates and nitrates," which are major inputs of the chemical industry, there were, nonetheless, "considerable salt deposits in Basel Land, Aargau and Valais."[12] Salt combined with water power provided a basis on which to build an electrochemical industry. The Swiss textile industry in the nineteenth century, though in large measure dependent on imports of cotton, nonetheless used indigenous silk from Ticino.[13] Similarly, the food-processing industry imported cocoa and sugar but used milk from Switzerland's substantial animal production.

Switzerland's fourth distinctive feature, its diverse population, has characterized the country for centuries. There are not only four official languages but also a variety of religions. Although these differences have led to opposing political preferences at times, notably during World War I, there have been no attempts at secession from the federation since 1847. It could be argued that the native population's diversity has made the country especially receptive to migration. At the beginning of the twentieth century, approximately 70 percent of the population spoke German, 21 percent spoke French, 6 to 8 percent spoke Italian, and slightly more than 1 percent spoke Romansch.[14] The German-speaking region at that time, as it has remained today, was in north, central, and east Switzerland; the French-speaking region was in the west; and the Italian-speaking region was in the south. Switzerland was also divided, as today, between Protestants and Catholics, with small minorities of Jews and other religions. Approximately 58 percent of the population was Protestant and 41 percent Catholic.[15] The cantons that were strongholds of Catholicism were in the south, namely, Valais and Ticino; in the central part of the country, namely, Uri, Obwalden, Nidwalden, Schwyz, Zug, Lucerne, Solothurn, and Fribourg; and one small half-canton in the northeast, Appenzell Inner-Rhoden. The mainly Protestant cantons were in the north, namely, Appenzell Ausser-Rhoden, Zurich, Schaffhausen, Basel-Country and Town, and Thurgau; in the west, namely, Vaud and Neuchâtel; and in the center, namely, Bern and Glarus. Geneva, Grisons, and Aargau were half Protestant and half

Catholic, and St. Gall, with a majority of Catholics, was still more than 40 percent Protestant.

Even though the geography of Switzerland differs from that of other European countries, the economic history during the late nineteenth and early twentieth centuries conformed to the rest of Western Europe. The depression of the 1880s affected Switzerland severely, leading to the largest recorded number of emigrants and to an agricultural crisis. The three years 1878, 1885, and 1894 were especially depressed,[16] as reflected in the decrease in exports, the decline in employment, and the reduction of real wages.[17] By 1890, the Swiss economy had largely recovered, and a new economic upswing, interrupted only by short-lived slumps from 1900 to 1903 and from 1907 to 1908, lasted until the outbreak of World War I.

Switzerland's employment structure underwent fundamental changes during the late nineteenth and early twentieth centuries. The number of people employed in industry surpassed the number employed in agriculture for the first time in the 1888 census. By 1910, the percentage of the population employed in the primary and tertiary sectors had nearly equalized at 27 percent, and the proportion employed in the secondary sector had reached 45.6 percent.[18]

The period of international free trade during the midnineteenth century was a prosperous one for the Swiss economy. After the cantons agreed to abolish internal customs duties in 1848, the country maintained a basically tariff-free trade policy. It successfully negotiated commercial treaties with Great Britain (1855), France (1865), the Austro-Hungarian Empire (1869), and the Customs Union of the German States (1870).[19] During these years, Switzerland was able to import industrial raw materials, such as coal, and manufactured products to supplement its small industrial base. Swiss textiles, watches, and food products enjoyed a healthy export market.

However, the reversion to protectionism in Germany in 1879 and the growing financial needs of the Swiss government led Switzerland to abandon liberal trade policies. Accordingly, in 1884, 1891, and 1902 tariffs were introduced. The protectionist policy favored some industries more than others and created problems with neighboring countries. The tariff war with France from 1892 to 1895, for instance, sharply reduced embroidery exports to France. Swiss agriculture, on the other hand, benefited from federal subsidies accorded to it. During the period of protection (1884 to 1914), annual trade deficits averaged 550 million Swiss francs, balanced by tourist receipts, interest on foreign investments, and other invisible earnings especially from banking and insurance.[20] Germany was the most important trading partner, followed by

France, Italy, Great Britain, Austria, and the United States. Industrial raw materials (that is, iron, coal, wool) came mainly from Germany; raw silk from Italy; cotton from Britain; grain from Russia and Austria; and sugar from Austria, France, and Germany.[21] At the outbreak of World War I, the leading Swiss exports in value were embroideries, watches, and silk goods.[22]

Not only did the Swiss economy become more protected and more industrialized during the quarter century before the First World War, but there were also visible signs of growing centralization. Politically, the twenty-two cantons had become more closely united in 1874 after revision of the federal constitution, which introduced significant changes in the organization of the army, legal system, educational provision, and direct democracy. By World War I, the cantons had handed over to federal government authority for the administration of post, currency, customs, telegraph, telephone, forests, and railroads.[23] Federal legislation had also attempted to equalize educational standards, working conditions in factories, agricultural and welfare benefits in all cantons.

An important demonstration of the increase of centralized power in the economy was the adoption of the Federal Factory Act in 1877. Although several individual cantons had enacted factory legislation before that time, the federal act has been considered by many Swiss historians to have strengthened considerably the federal government's influence with private industry. "It intervened deeply into industrial working conditions and represented a decisive first step by the federal government into social policy."[24] The provisions of the act were not in themselves revolutionary in comparison with legislation enacted in other countries during the late nineteenth century. The law stipulated an eleven-hour work day, forbad work on Sunday and employment in factories of children under fourteen, obligated the factory owner to assume responsibility for safety in the factory, and established a system of federal factory inspectors.

It is one of the contentions of this study that in order to abide by the provisions of this legislation, factory owners employed foreign labor either to supplement or replace traditional Swiss labor. As child labor was made illegal and the hours of work were reduced, employing foreign workers who could be paid lower wages became one way of maintaining production with rising manufacturing costs.

Related Migration Studies

Population movements that occurred in continental Europe before World War I have not been studied widely by scholars up to now.[25] By contrast, migrations of people from one continent to another, especially from Europe to North America, have been the subject of continual scholarly examination. Therefore, this study of intra-European migration has drawn heavily on analyses of intercontinental migration. Both the push and pull framework on which this book is based, as well as specific hypotheses, are closely related to previous research on the effects of intercontinental migration on economic growth.

Historians have long used the push and pull concept in analyzing motives for population movements. They have examined factors that have tended to push populations out of overly-populated countries and to pull them into those that are able to absorb additional population. Charlotte Erickson's recent collection of documents that describes rural problems in Germany, Sweden, Italy, Hungary, and Galicia during the nineteenth century illustrates one factor that induced emigration to the United States.[26] Wilbert Moore discussed at the end of World War II how "emigration might offer a quick solution" to population problems for countries in eastern and southern Europe. "Emigration is frequently proposed as a solution for major regional differentials in economic opportunity, and indeed has often been used as a source of release for crowded areas."[27] He went on to describe how emigration had been "a safety valve for eastern and southern European rural populations before the First World War."[28]

Historically, the push has been strongest in agricultural economies where the pressure of an increasing population has caused employment problems. However, the tendency to concentrate on agricultural conditions as the prime cause for the push has encouraged researchers to overlook industrial conditions.

Recent push and pull analyses that have made use of econometric methods have attempted to weigh the effect of several push and pull factors on migration to the United States.[29] One of the complexities in analyzing intra-European migration, however, has been that both push and pull factors existed within the same country. J. D. Gould has tried to relate the agricultural push to a competing phase of industrial development in the labor-exporting country. He described the counterattraction to emigration in those countries where there was "a growing industrial centre to compete with overseas destinations, such as around Stockholm, on the floor of the Po Valley, or in the central province of what had been Poland."[30]

Gould's most recent writings can be applied directly to the Swiss case. In the 1880s, Switzerland experienced mass emigration to the United States in unprecedented numbers.[31] Only a decade later, the Swiss economy itself was attracting migrants from Italy and southern Germany in substantial numbers. Therefore, Switzerland provides a good example of the complexities of push and pull factors existing side by side within the same economy.

Many studies of international population movements have examined the particular effect that migration has had on the development of industry in the receiving country. The conclusions reached in several of these studies have been similar to those found in this study. For instance, the first hypothesis of this book, that foreign workers provided a labor force for mass production, is a conclusion recognized by other researchers as a factor that contributed to industrial development in other countries as well.

The social effect of this role of migrant labor has been the focus of considerable research attention. Lenin, who himself was a foreign worker in Switzerland before World War I, was one of the first to mention the impact on society of foreign workers employed in large-scale industry. "Capitalism has created a particular sort of transmigration of peoples. Countries where industry develops rapidly, using machines to a greater extent and excluding backward countries from the world market, create salaries above the average and attract workers from less developed countries."[32] In his book *Imperialism, the Highest Stage of Capitalism,* Lenin described migration as part of imperialism. "One of the special features of imperialism . . . is the decline of the emigration from imperialist countries and the increase in immigration into these countries from the more backward countries where lower wages are paid."[33] This development, according to Lenin, tended to split the labor force in the imperialist countries. "Imperialism has the tendency to create privileged sections also among the workers, and to detach them from the broad masses of the proletariat."[34]

Stephen Castles and Godula Kosack developed this argument into a full-scale discussion of how foreign workers in Western Europe in the 1950s and 1960s fit into the class structure.

> Immigrant workers have a specific socio-economic function. They are recruited or admitted to Western European countries because they are willing to accept the least desirable jobs which have been deserted by indigenous labour. In objective terms, immigrant workers belong to the working class. But within this class they form the bottom stratum, due to the subordinate status of their occupations.[35]

Delia Castelnuovo-Frigessi, an Italian social scientist at the University of Lausanne, has used Lenin's writings as an "authentic model" for her description of the role of foreign workers in Switzerland today. She pointed to Lenin's description of migration to Switzerland: "The specific feature of imperialism in Switzerland is the increasing exploitation of foreign workers deprived of rights by the bourgeoisie of this country, who base their hopes on the division of the workers into two categories.[36]

Michael Piore, using an alternative vocabulary, has described a similar function for migrant labor. Analyzing migration flows into the United States before World War I, he stated that in a dual labor market, migrants are recruited for the secondary labor market, that is, the unsecured jobs.[37] "Migration was necessary," he wrote, "in order to man the lower rungs of the job hierarchy."[38]

The relationship of migration to industrial development has been studied not only from the vantage point of the labor market, but also in relation to the investment decision making of industries in the labor-importing countries.

Julius Isaac emphasized the positive relationship of migration to capital investment in industry by describing how "immigration tends to stimulate investment activities."[39] His analysis is applicable to the Swiss experience, even though his work was based on a study of intercontinental migration. He focused on the large-scale employment of migrants in U.S. mining and manufacture and discussed how the migration of both skilled and unskilled labor could "alter the state of technique."[40] The effect of skilled labor on the introduction of new technological investment was obvious, he wrote, for they "are able to improve the stock of technical knowledge in the receiving country."[41] However, the migration of unskilled labor could also affect the state of technique by encouraging the development of new inventions that "were generally not capital-saving but rather skilled labour-saving."[42] The use of this labor "was made possible only by the invention of new machines and the application of new processes, which largely reduced the amount of skill and experience formerly required."[43]

Brinley Thomas later developed this theme, showing how migration into the United States led to more capital intensive and automated methods of industrial production.

One of the chief reasons why America became the home of mass production and the pioneer of highly mechanized processes was that large periodic inflows of alien labour had made this evolution necessary. It was the technical price which had to be paid for effective and rapid economic assimilation; and one of its potent consequences was the development of a frame of mind—among workers as well as employers—alive to the advantages of scrapping out-of-date methods and adopting new techniques which increased productivity.[44]

This can be shown to have happened in Swiss industry as well. In several Swiss industries, the period from 1888 to 1914 was a transitional one, characterized by a change in production methods from cottage-based production to more automated factory production.[45] This was also a period of large-scale labor migration. The relationship between migration and capital investment was clearly demonstrated in the case of the embroidery industry when the introduction of automated machinery coincided with the employment of foreign workers.[46]

The second hypothesis, that foreign workers provided one linkage in the interdependent industrial development of Switzerland and Germany, is also a theme that has a theoretical relationship to other research, especially studies of regional industrialization in Europe.[47]

Several of the industrial centers in Switzerland were located near the country's borders; in fact, such centers as Basel, Geneva, St. Gall, Schaffhausen, and even Zurich could be described as European industrial centers rather than merely Swiss ones. In some cases, the region surrounding the Swiss industrial center was actually in another country, so that foreigners were actually part of the local work force. Therefore, movement into Switzerland from an area adjacent to a Swiss industrial center, although technically in another country, could be considered population movement within one region. When movements of capital as well as the import and export of raw materials and finished goods are considered as a whole, the interdependence of the industrial economies of southern Germany and northern Switzerland may provide a convincing example of regional industrial development.

If it can be established that the pattern of migration was intraregional, this study will perhaps advance the cause of regional studies of European industrial development. The fact that labor moved freely across European borders until the outbreak of World War I seems to strengthen the case for regionalization within the Continent.

2
WHO WERE THE FOREIGN WORKERS?

During the period between 1888 and 1914, the number of foreigners living in Switzerland increased from 229,650 or 7.9 percent of the total population to 600,000 or 15.4 percent of the total population.[1] At the same time, there was a "considerable net migration of Swiss citizens,"[2] which tended to accentuate the impact of large foreign population.

This chapter will describe five characteristics of the foreign population in Switzerland: gender, age distribution, country of origin, duration of stay in Switzerland, and geographical distribution. At the end of the chapter, a brief description of Swiss emigrants will be provided for comparison.

Although this study focuses on foreigners who came to Switzerland to work, the following demographic statistics describe all foreigners, whether employed or not. Nonetheless, the demographic profile presented in the chapter will help interpret push and pull factors which motivated the migration of labor. For instance, a nineteen-year-old, single Italian female who lived in St. Gall canton would have had different motives for coming to Switzerland than a forty-year-old, married German male who lived in the canton of Zurich.

Statistical data on which the chapter is based come from official censuses of Switzerland, 1888, 1900, and 1910. Many of the salient statistics have been reproduced or summarized in the *Statistisches Jahrbuch der Schweiz* (Statistical Yearbook of Switzerland) published annually since 1891. Data were collected in December; therefore, foreigners who came to Switzerland as seasonal workers in the spring and then returned to their own country in the autumn were not included in the figures.

Gender

The key question under examination here is to what extent the migration should be considered to have been male dominated. During the nineteenth century with massive overseas movements of population, the lone, young Scotsman, or Polish, German, or Italian male, who left home to seek employment in North or South America was a familiar figure. Similarly, intra-European migrations to mining regions in France, Germany, and Luxembourg were disproportionately male migrations.[3]

In the case of Switzerland, however, the preponderance of males was not so evident. According to the 1888 census, there were slightly more female foreigners than male foreigners living in Switzerland—115,040 females and 114,610 males.[4] By 1900, the number of foreign males had surpassed the number of foreign females, with males representing 52 percent of Switzerland's foreign population in both 1900 and 1910.[5]

Nonetheless, the male to female ratio was different for each foreign nationality group. The German population in Switzerland in 1910 was 52.5 percent female, whereas the Italian population was 58 percent male. The French were 54.7 percent female, and the Austrians were 52.5 percent male.[6] Regardless of nationality, the majority of both male and female migrants to Switzerland in the early twentieth century were unmarried. In 1900, 63 percent of the foreigners were single and in 1910, 62 percent.[7]

The existence of a substantial proportion of female foreigners in Switzerland before World War I suggests the range of roles played by foreigners in the Swiss economy. During the period from 1888 to 1914, female foreigners in Switzerland were especially important in two fields—the textile industry and as household servants.[8]

Age Distribution

Age of the foreign population is of especial interest for this study, since it is directly related to economic role. A migration disproportionately weighted toward prime working age (that is, 15–39 years) has more impact on the economy than a migration evenly distributed throughout all age groups.

In the case of Switzerland before World War I, raw population data show clearly that the largest proportion of foreigners, both male and female, was in the 15–39 age group.[9] In 1900 and 1910, approximately 52 percent of all foreigners were in that age group.

Another means of demonstrating that the foreign population was unusually or disproportionately skewed toward working-age migrants is by comparing the age distribution of foreign and Swiss populations. In the year 1910, significant differences existed between the two age distribution patterns. Only in the youngest age category (that is, 0–4 years) were the proportions of both populations equal. On the other hand, the foreign population was more heavily represented in working-age categories, whereas the Swiss population was more heavily represented in old-age categories.[10]

Country of Origin

Foreigners who came to Switzerland during the quarter century before World War I originated primarily from the four countries that surround Switzerland: France, Germany, the Austro-Hungarian Empire, and Italy.[11] During the midnineteenth century, the largest number of migrants had come from France, but by 1880, the number of Germans in Switzerland had far surpassed the number of French.[12] The French population in Switzerland remained relatively stable until the 1920s, when there was a notable decrease.[13] Furthermore, the vast majority of French nationals resided in western, French-speaking Switzerland.[14]

The largest contingent of foreigners living in Switzerland during the prewar period originated from Germany. The more than 200,000 Germans came mainly from southern Germany, Baden, and Württemberg, which share a common border with Switzerland. Smaller, though still considerable numbers of Germans came to Switzerland from Bavaria and Prussia.[15]

The movement of southern Germans to Switzerland may be viewed as part of a pattern of regional migration. The cultural and economic ties that linked German areas of Baden and Württemberg to the northern Swiss cantons were strengthened during the quarter century before World War I. This territory can be seen as having formed one industrial region, with labor migration taking place within the region.[16]

By the census of 1910, the number of Italians living in Switzerland had nearly equaled the number of Germans, amounting to 37 percent of the total number of foreigners. This had been a rapid growth, for in 1888 there were only 41,881 Italians in Switzerland.[17] Although there was a substantial migration of Italians to several European countries, nevertheless, Switzerland attracted the largest number of Italians within Europe during the early twentieth century.[18]

Italians in Switzerland originated for the most part from northern Italy—Lombardy, Venetia, and Piedmont.[19] However, unlike the Germans in Switzerland who stayed in the northern Swiss cantons, northern Italians did not necessarily remain in Ticino, the Italian-speaking canton that bordered Italy. In 1910, only 21 percent of the 200,000 Italians in Switzerland resided in Ticino, whereas 88 percent of the Germans resided in German-speaking cantons in Switzerland.[20] The mobility of Italians throughout the country in contrast to the comparative lack of mobility of Germans is one reason for the separate analyses of the two major nationality groups in this study. Migration of Italians to Switzerland has not been viewed as part of a regional industrialization process as was the case with German migration to Switzerland. Rather, motivations for Italian migration to Switzerland as well as the employment of Italian workers in the Swiss economy were more akin to overseas migrational patterns of Italians.[21]

The number of foreigners from the Austro-Hungarian Empire was insignificant in comparison with larger numbers of foreigners from Germany and Italy. Foreigners from Austria-Hungary who lived in Switzerland came mostly from the areas of the Vorarlberg and the Tirol, which border Switzerland in the east. Even though the number of Austrians was never large, nevertheless, it increased threefold during the period from 1888 to 1910.[22]

Duration of Stay

In order to analyze the overall impact that foreigners had on the Swiss economy, the length of stay of foreigners should be considered. It is convenient for this purpose to divide foreigners into categories according to how long they lived in the country. The tripartite description that will be used was suggested by a contemporary Swiss writer, who divided Italian migrants into three groups.[23]

The three categories were: seasonal workers, temporary workers, and permanent immigrants. This study is concerned mainly with foreigners in the second category—those who came to live in Switzerland for a few years. Temporary workers were also the most numerous and therefore had the strongest impact on the growth of the economy.

The first category describes any foreigner who came to Switzerland for any period less than one year. This would include, therefore, those who came in the spring and returned to their homeland in the autumn, even if they did this every year. Such a broad definition would also include those who did not actually live in Switzerland but crossed the border every day in order to work.

Foreigners in the first category originated mainly from Italy or Austria. Although the largest number of Austrian seasonal workers went to Germany, nevertheless, in the years immediately preceding World War I, Switzerland attracted a substantial number of them.[24] However, seasonal workers in Switzerland were primarily Italian. Before the turn of the century, the majority of Italians living in Switzerland had been in this category.[25]

Also included in the category of seasonal workers were foreigners who worked in Switzerland during the day and returned to their homeland each night. "Border-crossers" were not usually from Italy, but more frequently came from southern Germany or France. Although the specific number of workers is not known, nevertheless, several factories in both Geneva and Basel employed this foreign labor force.[26]

The number of foreign workers in the third category, permanent immigrants, also did not grow so rapidly as the total number of foreigners residing in Switzerland. One measure of permanency is the number of foreigners who acquired Swiss citizenship. Between 1889 and 1910, only 62,039 foreigners in Switzerland were naturalized.[27] This did represent some expansion, however, "from 5.5 percent of the total foreign population before 1900 to 8.3 percent shortly before World War I."[28]

During the period from 1889 to 1910, more Germans became Swiss citizens than did any other nationality of foreigner. There were 34,698 Germans naturalized during these years,[29] compared with only 7,738 Italians.[30] Yet as previously noted, by 1910, the number of Italian and German foreigners in Switzerland was nearly equal. There were even fewer foreigners from other countries who changed nationality during the period. However, in relation to the total number living in Switzerland, the French, Austro-Hungarians, Russians, and Americans had a comparatively high proportion of their nationals choosing Swiss citizenship.[31] The British, in contrast, "showed almost no interest in acquiring Swiss citizenship."[32]

The policies of the Swiss government on naturalization appear to have been in almost direct opposition to its policies on immigration. Doors were wide open to foreigners who wanted to live or work in the country but nearly shut to foreigners who wanted to acquire Swiss citizenship. This paradoxical situation was the subject of much controversy before World War I. Policies concerning naturalization of foreigners, however, were not new but based on long-standing Swiss law and tradition.

Citizenship in Switzerland, in contrast to most other countries, has been based on the origins of one's parents. A person born and raised in Switzerland, for example, is an alien if his or her parents are not Swiss citizens. Furthermore, responsibility for granting citizenship has traditionally resided with the local communities (that is, Gemeinde). Local jurisdiction has resulted in several kinds of abuses and in widely varying practices throughout the country. For instance, local governments, hesitant to accept people who might prove to be a financial burden, introduced heavy fees for naturalization. This practice has had the effect of permitting wealthy foreigners who may have lived in Switzerland for only a short time to acquire Swiss citizenship. On the other hand, less financially endowed foreigners who have lived in Switzerland all their lives have not be able to become Swiss nationals.

A Swiss federal law enacted in 1903[33] attempted to facilitate the naturalization of foreigners by delegating some responsibility in the matter to the federal government. However, it was left to the cantons whether or not to apply the new legislation. Swiss historians have concluded that the law had very little impact on extending Swiss citizenship to foreigners before the First World War. The law made it possible for foreigners to acquire a federal permit, but as Schlaepfer pointed out, this "granted neither the right to become citizens nor did it make one a citizen."[34]

Geographical Distribution

Since Switzerland is a country of widely varied geography, a closer examination of where foreigners lived will contribute directly to a fuller understanding of how they affected the Swiss economy. Attention will be focused on the regional distribution of foreigners within Switzerland, as well as on the urban and rural distribution of the foreign population. For the sake of comparison, the country has been divided into four regions according to the dominant language spoken: German, French, Italian (Ticino), and Romansch (Grisons).[35]

The German-speaking region of Switzerland attracted the largest number of foreigners. In 1910, more than 60 percent of all foreigners living in Switzerland resided in this region, whereas 26 percent resided in the French-speaking region, 8 percent in the Italian-speaking region, 8 percent in the Italian-speaking canton of Ticino, and 4 percent in Romansch-speaking Grisons.[36]

The explanation for this distribution of foreigners is clearly related to the expansion of the Swiss economy. During the two decades preceding World War I, the rapid growth of Swiss industry and other economic enterprises that employed foreign workers occurred to a larger extent in German-speaking Switzerland than elsewhere in the country.

It is interesting to dissect the regional statistics, examining the distribution of foreigners in individual cantons. Bickel has pointed out that three-quarters of all foreigners lived in only eight Swiss cantons, namely, Zurich, Bern, Basel-Town, St. Gall, Ticino, Vaud, Thurgau, and Geneva.[37] Within the German-speaking region, the cantons of Zurich, St. Gall and Basel-Town had the highest proportions of foreigners. In 1910, 20 percent of the population of Zurich canton, 17.5 percent of the population of St. Gall canton, and 37.5 percent of the population of Basel-Town were foreigners.[38] The canton of Basel-Town had maintained a large foreign population throughout the nineteenth century, so that the influx of foreigners during the prewar period was not a new phenomenon. Within the French-speaking region of Switzerland, the existence of a large foreign population in Geneva was traditional,[39] but the canton of Vaud also witnessed a rapid increase of foreigners during the period. In 1870, only 7 percent of the population of Vaud was foreign born, whereas by 1910, the proportion had risen to 14 percent. Grisons, the only Romansch-speaking canton, experienced a threefold increase in its foreign population during the period. Although there were some foreigners from Germany and Austria, by 1910, more than half of all foreigners in Grisons came from Italy.

Switzerland was not a strongly urbanized country before World War I, yet approximately half of all foreigners in the country lived in urban areas, defined in Switzerland as cities with more than 10,000 people. Cities in Switzerland were not only smaller than in most other industrialized countries, but they did not dominate the landscape. For instance, by 1910, only 25 percent of the total population of Switzerland lived in cities, a low figure in comparison with other European countries at the time.[40]

Similarly, in 1910, the largest cities in Switzerland were Zurich (population 190,733), Basel (population 132,276), and Geneva (population 130,917)—the only ones with more than 100,000 inhabitants.[41] In comparison, Paris, London, Berlin, Vienna, St. Petersburg, and Moscow had all surpassed the one million mark. Nevertheless, those three cities were large by Swiss standards, for in 1870, no city had yet reached a population greater than 50,000. Only in the last decade of the nineteenth and the first decade of the twentieth centuries could it be said that Switzerland had experienced an urbanization process.[42]

The other unusual aspect of Switzerland's urban growth was that industrial development was not necessarily connected to urbanization. Mayer has characterized Swiss cities as commercial rather than industrial.[43] "In so far as one can speak of actual factory towns in Switzerland, one would include small and medium-sized towns such as Winterthur or Baden and not the few large cities."[44] Nonetheless, around the turn of the twentieth century, workers' quarters did appear in Zurich, Basel, Lausanne, and Geneva.[45]

Foreigners living in Switzerland in the period before World War I inhabited not only the traditional border cities, such as Geneva and Basel, but also increasingly populated the more inland cities, such as Zurich, Lausanne, and St. Gall. In 1910, one-quarter of Lausanne's population and one-third of the inhabitants of Zurich and St. Gall were foreign born.[46] The rapid growth of foreigners in urban areas provoked discontent and even unrest among the indigenous population.[47]

It should be remembered, however, that half the foreigners in Switzerland did not live in cities.[48] They gravitated to the construction sites, tourist centers, and industries that were not necessarily located in urban areas. The attractiveness of particular regions and even cantons to foreigners can be directly related to employment opportunities. For instance, foreigners went to Grisons, where there was a substantial expansion of tourism; to St. Gall, where there was a considerable growth of the embroidery trade; and to Zurich, where there was a major development of the engineering industry.

Summary of Demographic Characteristics

Foreigners in Switzerland between 1888 and 1914 were both male or female, aged 15–39, and single. They originated from southern Germany or northern Italy and lived temporarily for a few years in the German-speaking region.

Swiss Emigration

During the nineteenth century, a large number of Swiss nationals emigrated from Switzerland. The population movement tended to peak during specific periods of economic adversity, such as the years from 1816 to 1819, 1851 to 1854, and the mid-1880s.[49] Hauser concluded that "Swiss tended to move abroad rather than to another canton."[50] They went mainly to the United States, where in 1910 there were 124,848 Swiss-born residents.[51]

At first, Swiss emigrants came primarily from rural areas in Switzerland and gravitated to midwestern farm states in the United States. However, by 1890, the destination of Swiss emigration changed. Grueningen noted that before 1890, Swiss "preferred to settle in rural communities of their own," and after this date, "Thousands of Swiss who had migrated from the rural sections, as well as new immigrants, formed colonies in the urban and industrial centers."[52] While the state of Ohio attracted the largest number of Swiss during the midnineteenth century, by 1890, the state of New York reported the largest contingent of Swiss-born residents, and by 1920, the state of California had the largest number of Swiss born.[53] The change in destination reflected a change in the character of Swiss emigration at the end of the nineteenth century. Mayer concluded that "nineteenth century emigration was predominantly agricultural, while twentieth century emigration has been primarily urban."[54]

Moreover, not all Swiss emigrants chose the United States as their destination. In the decade of the 1910s, according to the Swiss Federal Bureau of Emigration, 72 percent went to the United States, 17 percent to Latin America, and 3 percent to Canada.[55] Swiss emigration to Latin America and Canada continued during the interwar period when migration to the United States was restricted.

Swiss emigrants represented a cross section of the population, with the majority originating from the cantons of Ticino, central Switzerland (that is, Obwalden and Schwyz), and from Basel-Town. Until the mid-1880s, most Swiss emigrants had been farmers from mountain regions. After this period, Mayer had described construction workers from Ticino and Grisons; industrial workers, technicians, businessmen, and clerks from the cities; and teachers and governesses from French-speaking regions as well represented among emigrants.[56] During the period from 1887 to 1938, Lobsiger estimated that approximately 33 percent of Swiss emigrants were farmers, 27 percent were in industrial occupations, 11 percent in commerce, 8 percent in personal service, 6 percent in professions, and 4.5 percent in tourism.[57] Lobsiger's statistical study of Swiss emigrants concluded that they were mainly male (62 percent), single (72.5 percent), and aged 20–39 years (59 percent).[58]

Emigration from Ticino was especially sizable throughout the nineteenth century. Between 1843 and 1873, for example, 12 percent of the total cantonal population emigrated.[59] Emigrants were attracted to northern California, where the Italian Swiss colony created a grape-growing business of economic significance. In addition, Australia was the destination for a substantial number of Ticinese during the first half of the nineteenth century.

Motivations for Swiss emigration overseas are difficult to identify in light of the substantial migration of foreigners into Switzerland during a similar time period. Nonetheless, it is worth emphasizing that in fact "the quantitative importance of Swiss emigration diminished after 1890."[60] Therefore, Swiss emigration from a chronological viewpoint could be said to have predated the large-scale influx of foreigners into Switzerland. However, emigration on a smaller scale continued into the twentieth century. One feasible explanation for the continuation is the inherent diversity of Switzerland, which may explain why a Catholic, Italian-speaking Swiss might consider moving to a German-speaking, Protestant canton more disruptive than moving to an Italian section of New York City, even though the United States is several thousand miles further away.

3
MOTIVATIONS FOR MIGRATING TO SWITZERLAND

Since the vast majority of foreigners who worked in Switzerland between 1888 and 1914 originated from either Germany or Italy, we have to examine their countries of origin to understand why they came. This chapter will look first at reasons for a population movement from Germany to Switzerland and then in part 2 at the movement from Italy to Switzerland.

The two migrations, although simultaneous, had quite distinct motivations. In the case of Germans, migration represented by and large a movement away from a rapidly industrializing region to a more traditional economy in Switzerland. In the case of Italians, the Swiss economy offered a more quickly expanding labor market than their own country was providing.

Nonetheless, in the case of both Germans and Italians, motivations combined both push and pull factors. This chapter will concentrate on features of the German economy and society and of the Italian economy and society that tended to push populations out of their homelands. Other chapters will focus more specifically on attractions of the Swiss economy that acted as a pull to Germans and Italians.

Migration from Germany

During the quarter century before World War I, Switzerland progressively became a more popular destination for Germans. Not only skilled mechanics, tailors, physicians, and brewers, but also female servants and intellectuals, such as Einstein and Hesse, were attracted to Switzerland.

The population movement during this period was not an entirely new phenomenon. Traditionally, some Germans had migrated to Switzerland, although in smaller numbers. In 1860, for instance, nearly fifty thousand Germans lived in Switzerland.[1] At the end of the nineteenth century and during the first decade of the twentieth century, the number of Germans living in Switzerland expanded rapidly, increasing from 112,342 in 1888 to 219,530 in 1910.[2]

Germans who migrated to Switzerland came predominantly from southwest Germany, that is, Baden and Württemberg. In fact, economic and social connections between this region of Germany and northern Switzerland have been so long lasting and intensive that it is difficult to discuss the movement solely as a migration of population. It would, perhaps, be more pertinent to place the population movement in a larger framework of regional development, including the movement of capital and technology. This point will be elaborated later. However, it is also necessary to place the migration of Germans to Switzerland within the larger context of emigration from Germany, remembering that during the nineteenth century, approximately four million Germans emigrated to the United States.[3] The outflow continued until World War I, although the last peak of overseas emigration took place during the 1880s.[4]

The growth of the movement of people from Germany to Switzerland occurred, for the most part, after the mass overseas migration had somewhat curtailed. Between 1894 and 1910, only 380,907 Germans emigrated to countries overseas in North and South America and Australia,[5] whereas in Switzerland alone in 1910, there were more than 200,000 Germans.

To complicate the story further, the population movement to Switzerland, although small in comparison with nineteenth-century mass movements, took place at a time of German economic growth and expansion. Even in southwest Germany, cities and industries were undergoing rapid transformation. As Schadt and Schmierer recently described, "Stuttgart and Mannheim developed during this time into the centers of the most important agglomeration regions of southwest Germany."[6]

Stuttgart, by 1912, had a population of 290,000, which was far in excess of any Swiss city at the time.[7] The industrialization of the Stuttgart region progressed rapidly from 1882 and was based primarily on the production of consumer goods, metalworking, electrical machinery, and printing. Traditional industries, such as textiles, were superceded during this period by the engineering and metalworking industries. For example, the well known giant enterprises, Daimler motors and Bosch auto electronics, were founded in the decades preceding World War I.

The Stuttgart region in fact attracted its own foreign labor. By 1914, as the fourteenth most industrialized city in Germany and the one with the highest wages, foreigners from Tirol, Italy, Bohemia, and Styria, as well as Hungary, Poland, and Galicia came to the region to work.[8]

Mannheim, which was the largest city in Baden, also experienced a period of extensive growth during these years. From a city with a population of 53,000 in 1880, it had nearly quadrupled in number to 193,000 by 1910. However, the expansion cannot be ascribed to industrial development alone, for Mannheim maintained a strong position as a shipping, trade, and transportation center. As the second most important inland German harbor,[9] opportunities for banking and insurance services brought employment possibilities "well beyond the average town."[10]

It was in the industrial sector, however, that the numbers of jobs most increased. "The machine construction (Benz built the first car there in 1885) had already in the '80s, together with rubber, wood pulp and chemicals . . . made Mannheim the most important industrial area of Baden."[11]

Mannheim and Stuttgart, though the largest centers of industrialization, were not the only towns where south Germans could find employment. In a myriad of smaller towns in both Baden and Württemberg, such as Karlsruhe, Heidelberg, Konstanz, Freiburg, Pforzheim, and Friedrichshafen, opportunities for employment were also increasing. The region surrounding Stuttgart, including the middle Neckar Valley and the Fils River valley, became especially industrialized.

In the midst of such economic activity, how can people's motivations for leaving be explained? Furthermore, why did those opting to leave choose Switzerland as their destination? The motives for the population movement may be described as a combination of push and pull factors.

Those occupational groups of Germans who were unable or unwilling to participate in the general growth of industry could be said to have been pushed out of Germany. Germans whose traditional livelihoods were increasingly threatened by the industrialization of southwest Germany began to react strongly in the early 1890s. David Blackbourn has described how their grievances were expressed politically through the growth of the Center party. However, another expression of reaction against "deep-seated economic and social grievances"[12] was the migration of many of these threatened people to Switzerland. The population movement was a push out of Germany of medium-sized farmers, artisans, and shopkeepers.

Not only economic factors but political factors as well pushed some Germans out of Germany. Those interested in trade union or political activity or those merely opposed to aspects of prewar German society found "Switzerland in spite of police attacks, more liberal than the neighboring foreign country."[13]

Germans were not entirely motivated to migrate to Switzerland by negative reactions to Germany; on the contrary, a variety of reasons attracted or pulled Germans to Switzerland. In some cases, the Swiss economy offered easier access to occupations that were difficult to pursue in Germany. In other cases, socio-economic ties between southern Germany and Switzerland were so well established that it was more natural to move south across the Swiss border than to another region of Germany.[14] Since this chapter is concerned primarily with explaining the population movement from southwest Germany to Switzerland, it focuses on the predominant group from Baden and Württemberg, although many of the motives presented here could apply to other Germans.

One group of migrants to Switzerland came from the agricultural sector. Not only were farmers abandoning agriculture during the late nineteenth century, but families of farmers were also leaving rural areas. Female domestic servants in Switzerland in 1910 came mainly from rural areas in Württemberg and Bavaria.[15] In order to understand the changing fate of the farmer in southwest Germany during prewar years, it is necessary to examine the history of agricultural settlement. Farm land in both Baden and Württemberg had long been noted for parcellation. The small-sized holdings have often been mentioned as motivation for mass emigration to the United States in the midnineteenth century.

> The districts where the land is subdivided to a great extent, were those which suffered the most severely in the six years from 1849 to 1855, inasmuch as the population of fifteen districts where the land is, without exception, held by small proprietors, was reduced from 400,000 in 1849 to 360,000 in 1855, being a diminution of 10 per cent, and from these districts the larger number of emigrants proceeded.[16]

Nonetheless, not all agricultural land in Baden and Württemberg had been fragmented.[17] Those areas that were Catholic, such as the Black Forest and Upper Swabia, but also some Protestant regions, such as Hohenlohe and parts of the Swabian Alps north of the Danube River had resisted the practice of excessive subdivision. Instead, landholdings had been passed down through the system of primogeniture. Farms there tended to be larger, and until the last quarter of the nineteenth century, they had prospered.

However, the agricultural crisis that hit European agriculture in general also affected the previously successful farmers of southwest Germany. As Blackbourn has noted, "These areas now paid the price for earlier success in resisting debt, foreclosure and rural exodus."[18] The problems that they now faced were different from any they had experienced in the past. No longer were harvest failures or the weather the primary complaints. The new problem was international competition in grain and animal produce made possible by the steamship and railways. To make matters worse, the government of the industrializing economy was no longer particularly concerned about the farmer's plight. Rising costs of production, higher rates of taxation, scarcity of credit, and the Caprivi trade treaties were all problems that a more sympathetic government could have ameliorated. But as Blackbourn concluded, "There was a slackening of that solicitude which governments had formerly shown towards agriculture."[19]

Farmers in southwest Germany shared all these problems. In Baden and Württemberg, production of grains (especially spelt, oats, and barley) and legumes comprised more than half of the harvest in 1880.[20] The rest of the farming consisted of meat and dairy production and the cultivation of special crops, such as hops, vines, and tobacco. By the early 1890s, most of these types of farmers faced difficulties. The prices of hops, grains, barley, and oats fell disastrously. Livestock suffered from severe outbreaks of foot and mouth disease, as well as shortages of animal feeds. Because tariff rates were reduced in 1890 and 1894, German production of oats, barley, oxen, calves, meat, and hops was less competitive than imports.[21] Some of the rural population in southwest Germany reacted to these problems by abandoning its farms. Farmers were attracted to Switzerland as a solution to their problem; some entered the agricultural sector in Switzerland,[22] but others found in migration an opportunity to change occupation. The Swiss economy provided a more traditional atmosphere where people could enter into the industrial or service sectors.

In addition to farmers who felt increasingly pushed out of their livelihoods in southwest Germany by industrialization, certain categories of craftsmen and shopkeepers were subjected to similar pressures. Switzerland had always been a stopping-off place for carpenters, mechanics, and bookbinders. Germans had traditionally spent a few years in Swiss industry, and some had settled there because of marriage to a Swiss woman.[23]

During the quarter century before World War I, even though Swiss industry was rapidly becoming factory based and machine production orientated, German artisans still frequently found a place. According to the 1905 industrial census, 7,305 Germans were employed as independent manufacturers. Prominent in this group were shoemakers, tailors, carpenters, and bakers.

Reinhard Rigling from Watterdingen in Germany was such an immigrant.[24] He came to Switzerland in 1894 as a journeyman carpenter and started a wood-processing firm in Oerlikon (part of Zurich) the next year. He became a Swiss citizen in 1910. Christian Stoos, the son of a prosperous Württemberg farmer, was another example of such a German foreign worker.[25] He came to Zurich as a skilled blacksmith, married a Swiss woman, and founded his own hoof and wagon blacksmith's shop in 1905 in Zurich. In the food-processing industry, Karl Ziegler was an example of a German butcher from Stuttgart who started a butcher's shop in Switzerland.[26] He learned the butcher's trade at his parents' restaurant and butcher business in Germany, came to Zurich in 1899, and married a Swiss woman.

German small businessmen came to Switzerland for a variety of motives, a combination of push and pull factors. The disadvantages that they faced as artisans or shopkeepers in southern Germany and the comparative advantages offered by the Swiss economy provided the major motivations.

To some extent, the problems small businessmen faced in southern Germany were related to the agricultural crisis. The financially strapped farmers could not generate sufficient demand to purchase goods that artisans produced and sold. Yet during the same period, the number of retail shops in southwest Germany expanded rapidly,[27] increasing competition for a decreasing number of customers.

Perhaps more critical for the family shoemaker or carpenter was competition from large, factory-based concerns. According to Blackbourn, small businesses "were mostly unable to take advantage of economies of scale, their share of the available capital stock was shrinking and they frequently had problems competing for raw materials and outlets."[28] Under the circumstances, the only way for an artisan to maintain his position as self-employed was to contract to a larger firm or concentrate more on repairs than on manufacturing.

In some of the fields in which Germans were finding survival as small businessmen most precarious, Switzerland offered a more amenable economic climate. For instance, factory production of ready-made clothing was very slow to begin in Switzerland.[29] German tailors found it relatively easy to practice their trade in Swiss, German-speaking cities. During the prewar period, wood was not usually processed in a factory in Switzerland;[30] thus German carpenters were still able to establish workshops, and by 1905, 1,053 were listed as self-employed in Switzerland.[31] Beer brewing was another field into which Germans had long had easy access: Approximately one-third of all people in the brewery business in Switzerland in 1905 was German, for instance. Yet Blackbourn has emphasized the problems of family breweries in southwest Germany because of a "market dominated by a number of large firms utilising technical innovations."[32]

However, the population movement from southwest Germany to Switzerland should not be viewed exclusively as one of farmers and small businessmen pushed out of traditional occupations. The largest numbers of migrants from Germany were employed in Swiss factories or service occupations. How can this be explained? During the very period when German industries were demanding more workers, some Germans chose to work in Swiss industries rather than German ones.

In the following discussion, it will be shown to what extent the population movement could be considered part and parcel of internal migration movements. At the same times and for the same reasons that people moved into industrial centers in Baden or Württemberg, others moved to industrial centers in northern Switzerland. Traditional economic and cultural links between southwest Germany and Switzerland were so strong that crossing the border to live was not distinguishable from internal migration.

It could be argued that southwest Germany and German-speaking Switzerland were part of one economic and social region. Author Hermann Hesse, who lived during his lifetime in Württemberg (Calw), in Baden (Gaienhofen on Lake Constance), and in Switzerland (Basel and Bern), expressed that attitude about the region:

> This southwest German-Swiss area is home to me, and although it was made often enough exceedingly clear to me that several state borders and one national border run through this area, I, however, have never in my inner most feelings been able to perceive these borders as natural. For me, home was on both sides of the Upper Rhine, whether the country was called Switzerland, Baden or Württemberg.[33]

Furthermore, a common spoken language helped merge the areas into one cultural region: The colloquial language spoken in Baden, Württemberg, and northern Switzerland is a similar dialect of German.

The strongest economic link that united the region was the central position of the city of Basel. As it grew into an important industrial, trade, and banking center during the nineteenth century, the workforce came not only from Swiss territory to the east and south of the city but also from Baden in the north.

Germans had always comprised a large percentage of the city's population. As Paul Burckhardt wrote, "In 1870 the number of foreigners already comprised 30 percent of the population. In the following years more foreigners streamed in, partly from Alsace, but predominantly from Germany from neighboring Baden. There were years, when in Kleinbasel, two-thirds of the inhabitants were Germans."[34] Germans from Baden continued to migrate more to Basel than to any other Swiss canton.[35]

Basel's industries, especially chemicals and textiles, had long benefited from close connections with neighboring Baden. Chemical firms had employed foreign workers from the nearby countryside, set up subsidiaries there, and exchanged technology.[36] The textile industry and in particular two specialized branches associated with Basel, the manufacture of silk ribbons and lace borders, had also employed a large contingent of German workers.

Silk ribbon manufacture had originally been organized as a system of outwork production. Entrepreneurs, called "Bändelherren" in Basel, had supplied silk thread to weavers in cottages outside the city. Included in the system were cottage weavers located in southern Baden, Germany. Wilhelm Bocks mentioned that the Basel firm Gesellschaft für Bandfabrikation owned weaving machines and supplied raw materials to homeworkers living in Säckingen, Baden, into the twentieth century.[37] By the midnineteenth century, however, silk ribbons started to be manufactured in factories in Basel as well. Homeweavers from the countryside were attracted to the factories because of the potential of increased earnings. According to Martin Schaffner, between 1840 and 1880, "Thousands of people especially from the canton of Basel Country and from the duchy of Baden migrated in order to seek work in the silk ribbon industry."[38] Using factory statistics of 1888, he traced the origins of textile workers as far north as the upper Black Forest region, including Freiburg, and as far east as Waldshut, Baden.[39]

However, economic connections between southwest Germany and Switzerland were not confined to the unique situation of Basel. Throughout the nineteenth century, the two economies became more and more intertwined. Swiss firms, such as Honegger's textile factories in Kempten (in Allgäu, western Bavaria) and Escher Wyss's paper machinery plant in Ravensburg (Württemberg), were established in order to take advantage of a larger German market. German firms, on the other hand, crossed the border into Switzerland to gain more access to the world market and safeguard their industries in neutral territory in case of war.[40] Industrial links sometimes led directly to the movement of workers.

Heilwig Schomerus in an intensive study of a Württemberg engineering firm, Maschinenfabrik Esslingen, pointed out the existence of regional-workers exchanges in the engineering industry. The area Schomerus examined was within a radius of 200 to 300 kilometers and included engineering factories in Karlsruhe, Nürnberg, Augsburg, Zurich, and Esslingen, which is in the Stuttgart area. Especially during the period between 1897 and 1914, Schomerus found evidence of large numbers of skilled mechanics, lathe operators, and blacksmiths moving within this region.[41]

Growing trade contacts also connected the two economies. Trade in agricultural produce developed through the Lake Constance port of Friedrichshafen, linking the farmland of Upper Swabia in Württemberg with the industrializing canton of St. Gall and Thurgau in Switzerland. As Basel acquired the status of a Rhine River port in 1906, a large trade in coal and other raw materials reached Switzerland from the north.

Imports from Germany increased substantially during the period from 1892 to 1912.[42] Thirty-two percent of all imported raw materials, food and manufactured goods to Switzerland were of German origin by 1912. Manufactured goods were the most important category of Swiss imports from Germany, but raw materials, such as iron, coal, leather, and wool, were also imported mainly from Germany. Food imports from Germany, though not so significant in quantity nor value, accounted for 12 percent of total Swiss food imports by 1912. Sugar was the major food import, but a variety of agricultural imports produced in southwest Germany provided supplies of food, especially for northern Swiss cities.

Swiss exports to Germany were not so substantial, comprising only one-half the value of imports.[43] By 1912, 22 percent of total Swiss exports were sold to Germany. Although the total value of Swiss exports to Germany had increased, during these years, Germany because a somewhat less important market for Swiss goods measured in volume. For instance, although in 1892, 22 percent of Swiss food exports had gone to Germany, by 1912, Germany's share had fallen to only 15 percent of total Swiss food exports. In raw materials and manufactured goods, the comparative role of the German market for Swiss exports had remained relatively stable.

For Germans intellectually or politically opposed to German society, Switzerland had traditionally offered an accessible alternative home. During the revolutions of 1848–49, several of the most active and therefore most sought after Germans had fled to Switzerland.[44] Richard Wagner, escaping arrest after participating in the Dresden Uprising of 1849, spent the next nine years in Zurich. During the lifetime of Bismarck's antisocialist law (1878 to 1890), numerous German socialists were able to continue political activities in Zurich. German revolutionaries at one time or another, such as Georg Büchner, Ferdinand Freiligrath, Wilhelm Weitling, August Bebel, Gustav Landauer, Willi Münzenberg, and Erich Mühsam, had all sought refuge in Switzerland.[45]

During the quarter century preceding World War I, Switzerland continued to attract Germans with intellectual or political motivation. Some of these people tried to use the relative safety of the country as a base for effecting future change in their homeland. Others adopted Switzerland because they were attracted to a society where "the spirit of militarism is singularly absent."[46] Albert Einstein, who became a Swiss citizen in 1901, was one of those Germans intellectually attracted to the country: "He enjoyed the Swiss with their mixture of serious responsibility and easy going democracy, their refusal to be drawn into the power game already dividing Europe, their devotion to a neutrality which was personal as well as political."[47]

At this time, Switzerland had become a home for discontented foreigners from many parts of Europe: Poles, Romanians, Hungarians, and Russians made use of the open migration laws and the opportunities to study. Rosa Luxemburg, a German politician of Polish descent, the Russian politician Alexandra Kollontai, and the Romanian politician Anna Pauker all studied at the University of Zurich. Geneva became an international gathering place for political Russians in the two decades before the Russian Revolution.[48] Lenin and his wife, Nadezhda Krupskaya, lived there from 1900 to 1905, as did the earlier generation of Russian revolutionaries, such as G. V. Plekhanov, Vera Zasulich, and Paul Axelrod.

Although the number of Germans who came to Switzerland for political or intellectual reasons did not compare with those who came for purely economic motivations,[49] nonetheless the impact that these foreigners had on Swiss society was considerable. The fear of *Überfremdung* (foreign domination), which was widespread in the early 1900s, was connected in some ways to the influence of these political migrants. Many who personally rejected their German background attempted to participate fully in Swiss society through the trade union movement or directly through Swiss political parties. Particularly noteworthy in this respect were Hermann Greulich, Emil Beck, Karl Manz, and Robert Seidel, all who were born in Germany and became Swiss citizens and political leaders in Switzerland.

Hermann Greulich, born in 1842 in Breslau, arrived in Switzerland in 1865 as a journeyman bookbinder. Active in the Swiss worker's movement until his death in 1925, he has been named the "first professional social democrat politician in Switzerland."[50] Emil Beck, who was born in Baden in 1848, came to Switzerland when he was thirteen and learned the tailor's trade. He rose to the position of secretary of the government committee of the Swiss Trade Union Federation. Karl Manz fled from Berlin in the 1880s and held the position of president of the Social Democratic party of canton Zurich for twelve years. Robert Seidel, who became a Swiss citizen at the age of thirty in 1880, was elected to the National Council (parliament).

Perhaps more significant were the political Germans who lived in Switzerland but directed their activity toward change in Germany. Between 1879 and 1888, the newspaper *Sozialdemokrat* (the organ of the German Social Democratic party) was written and printed in Zurich and secretly distributed in Germany. Such renowned names in German socialist history as Georg von Vollmar, Eduard Bernstein, Leonhard

Tauscher, Friedrich Schülter, and Karl Kautsky were involved with the publication at one time or another.[51] Later in 1898 and 1906, Germans living in Basel and Schaffhausen crossed the border to help in election campaigns of German social democrats. The socialist Willi Münzenberg was also able to make good use of his stay in Switzerland to further the cause of international socialism. Between 1910, when he arrived in Zurich to work in Josef Apotheke, and 1918, when the police escorted him to the border, he organized an international socialist youth movement.[52]

Migration from Italy

Italians who came to Switzerland to work from 1888 to 1914 originated primarily from the north of Italy—from Lombardy, Piedmont, or Venetia.[53] Marrocchi has shown that Italians who migrated within Europe rather than overseas came for the most part from the northeast (that is, Trentino Alto-Adige, Veneto, Friuli, and Emilia-Romagna) and the northwest (that is, Piemonte, Val D'Aosta, Lombardia, and Liguria).[54] Switzerland received the largest number of intra-European-migrating Italians during the first decade of the twentieth century. However, Germany, France, and Austria-Hungary also attracted a substantial number of Italian foreign workers.[55] They were part of the mass Italian emigration movement, which, between the years 1876 and 1915, amounted to fourteen million people. Approximately half emigrated within Europe, and half went overseas to North and South America.[56]

Population data demonstrate very clearly that emigration from northern Italy was substantial, but data do not give motives for the emigration, which are not readily apparent. Historians have usually described the northern part of Italy as a prospering, rapidly industrializing region in the decades before World War I. The textile and engineering industries in Lombardy and Piedmont were especially reputed to be successful competitors in the international market place. The Po Valley was as rich and as technologically advanced an agricultural area as anywhere in Europe; why then did northern Italians come to Switzerland?

Historians have focused attention on primarily economic problems that made life difficult in Italy and motivated inhabitants to look across the border to find employment. However, while economic conditions were often depressed in northern Italy, as discussion will show, it is not clear that the only alternative was emigration. Could not the potential labor of the mountain peasant or the unemployed builder been used in the growing industry of northern Italy? The contention here is that the Italian government actually encouraged emigration for a variety of economic and political reasons. Emigration to Switzerland, in particular, was encouraged as a traditional destination for northern Italians.

For centuries, northern Italy had been connected economically to the rest of Europe. In the case of Italy and Switzerland, there had been important exchanges of capital and expertise in the textile industry as far back as the sixteenth century. Swiss firms operated branches in Italy, and Italian entrepreneurs had played a major role in developing silk manufacture in Zurich. During the nineteenth century, when the pace of industrialization quickened with the construction of the railroad and the growth of factories, Swiss capital and Swiss companies spread into northern Italy. For example, Honegger, a textile machinery enterprise in Rüti in canton Zurich, had a branch in Bergamo in Lombardy; Brown Boveri, the engineering firm, set up a subsidiary in Milan soon after its founding in Switzerland in 1891.

Switzerland had been an educational center for wealthy Italians throughout the nineteenth century. The department store entrepreneur Ferdinando Bocconi sent his sons to study there. Luigi Burgo of the paper industry completed his studies in Switzerland,[57] and the political leader, Cavour, took study trips to Switzerland.

From the mountain villages of northern Italy emigration to Switzerland had been a customary way of life:

> In some communes, especially of Como and Bergamo, certain trades are traditional, such, for example, as that of the mason, or stone cutter, or porter, or brazier, or potter; and whoever takes up one of these with the intention of emigrating knows for a certainty that he will have the support of the masters of his place who have preceded him . . . and will gladly enroll him in their troop or at least help him and steer him in his first ventures.[58]

Josef Brosi was such an Italian migrant to Switzerland.[59] Trained as a construction worker in his home town of Como, he first worked as a foreman at a large building firm in Zurich. In 1908, he started his own building materials business in Zurich. Unlike the majority of Italian migrants to Switzerland, however, he did not return to Italy.[60]

According to an Italian government inquiry in 1888, "The fundamental and most widespread cause of emigration was poverty, not only in the South but also in Lombardy, Emilia and the Veneto."[61] If this indeed was the primary motivation for migration to Switzerland, a hypothesis to be scrutinized later, what evidence was there of poverty in northern Italy?

During the quarter century before World War I, Italy was experiencing rapid growth in population, due mainly to a recent fall in the mortality rate. After unification (in the 1860s), national mortality rates continued to average as high as thirty people per thousand, declining to twenty people per thousand at the outbreak of World War I. Average rates in northern Italy fell somewhat faster than in the south.[62] The phenomenon was by no means unique to Italy, for Switzerland, in accord with most Western European countries, had also witnessed a substantial decrease in the death rate during the latter part of the nineteenth century. In fact, Italy's mortality statistics continued to be somewhat higher than those in the rest of Europe.[63] As del Panta described, "Around 1890 serious infectious diseases were significantly more widespread than in other European countries."[64] Yet it should be noted that southern Italy registered far more deaths from malaria, typhoid fever, measles, and diphtheria than did northern Italy. Tuberculosis, which was the most prevalent cause of death in the country as a whole, however, was more frequent in northern Italy. This disease was a common cause of death throughout Europe during the period, illustrating the general correspondence of northern Italy's population composition with that of the Continent.

Changes in Italy's birth rate also conformed to European patterns, although here again, statistics average slightly higher than those for other more northern countries.[65] The decline in the birth rate, however, began in the 1890s, which was somewhat earlier than in Switzerland yet later than in Britain.[66]

Therefore, Italy's population profile during the three decades before World War I was not exceptional enough to have been the prime cause of its poverty. The population in other European countries, notably Germany, was increasing at faster rates. However, in the case of Italy, in contrast to other Western European countries, the economy was not able to absorb the increasing population. Even when the Italian economy experienced very rapid growth, during the period from 1896 to 1908,[67] "the supply of labor exceeded jobs of the quality which was demanded."[68] The limitations of the economy are said to have affected employment prospects in three specific areas, namely, in agriculture, manufacturing, and jobs for women. It will be shown to what extent these limitations provided motivation for emigration.

The agricultural depression of the 1880s, which affected most countries in Europe, struck Italy's mainly agricultural economy especially hard. In 1881, 51.4 percent of the population were employed in agriculture, a figure that did not decline until the 1930s.[69] The depression hit capitalist and peasant farms alike—the large grain landholdings in the Po Valley as well as the olive, vegetable, and stock smallholdings in the mountains. In Mantua, an agricultural center in the Po Valley in Lombardy, there was "a long and bitter strike" of agricultural laborers in 1884.[70] Traditional centers of silk production, such as Como in Lombardy and Cuneo in Piedmont, suffered when Crispi's government refused to renew the trade agreement with France in 1888, thereby cutting off the main export market for silk. Problems in the agricultural sector were long lasting, for the last few years of the century (1896 to 1900) were also poor farming years, with "the bad harvest in 1897 bringing the threat of famine to many areas."[71]

Farmers who migrated to Switzerland from northern Italy during the 1880s, 1890s, and the first decade of the twentieth century came from small subdivided, often mountain farms.[72] In the mountainous region, which extends along the border with Switzerland, and even in the hilly countryside of northern Lombardy and Piedmont, farms were usually very small: "The large majority of which extend to less than one hectare in size."[73] It was on these farms, subdivided church or communal lands, that a farmer tried to produce crops from rocky, infertile soil, using only the most basic ploughs and harrows. The father of Pietro Bianchi, who was an migrant worker in Switzerland, was one of these peasant farmers on Lake Como.[74] He cultivated a smallholding of grapevines, the income from which was insufficient to provide for his family. In the hilly region of upper Milan, silk was the main crop produced on small farms at the end of the nineteenth century. Peasant life, including children's school attendance, revolved around crop requirements: from the moment co-coon raising started, the number of children at school fell markedly.[75] During the last years of the nineteenth century, expropriations of such small farmers, unable to meet mortgage or tax payments, were very high, amounting to 82,069 farmers throughout Italy between 1885 and 1897.[76]

Not all migrants to Switzerland from northern Italy came from peas-ant farms: Industrial workers also emigrated; yet there is no evidence of decreased job opportunities in industrial employment in northern Italy in the late nineteenth century. On the contrary, most historians have pointed to the period as one of rapid industrial growth, concentrated for the most part (even disproportionately) in the north of Italy. Lombardy, in particular, has often been cited as a prime example of an industrializ-ing region. Why then did northern Italians leave to work in industrial enterprises in Switzerland when the number of industrial jobs was increasing rapidly in their homeland? The customary explanation has been the "limited absorption capacity of the internal labour market."[77] Although industrial jobs were expanding, the number was still insuffi-cient to include all potential workers. Yet this explanation seems inade-quate in light of the very substantial industrial development that did take place.

The Lombard city of Milan, which, according to Foerster, "was the chief industrial section of Italy,"[78] grew measurably, doubling in popula-tion between unification and the turn of the century.[79] Industrial growth was rapid and extensive, as described in a recent study of the city's growth between 1859 and 1892. Large-scale factories, such as Pirelli's rubber enterprise, Falck's steel works, and Ernesto Breda's machine shop, were to be found, as well as sweatshops for manufacturing clothing.

In addition to the Milan region, the textile industry was expanding elsewhere in northern Italy during the several decades before World War I. Manufacture of cotton cloth, which was concentrated in Lombardy along the many rapidly flowing rivers, went through a period of modernization.[80] A number of family businesses were incorporated from the 1870s, capital expenditure tripled between 1900 and 1908, and by the beginning of World War I, many of the medium-sized firms that were dominant in the cotton textile industry had joined together to form two powerful cartels. Wool production in northern Italy also expanded. By 1914, Italy was able to meet its home demand for wool and to produce a small excess for export, whereas in 1871, the country had imported half of its woolen requirements.

Furthermore, there was a substantial increase in the production of building materials, especially Portland cement. The largest concentration of firms was in Lombardy as well, in the provinces of Bergamo and Como. In newer industries, such as the electrical industry, "Italy was one of the pioneers,"[81] which led to the early development of an electrical equipment industry.

Yet it was the ferrous metallurgy and engineering industries that were "the leading sectors of Italian industrialization."[82] In the development of the Milan region, this sector played a dominating role, employing the largest number of industrial workers in the most technologically advanced enterprises.[83] According to Hunecke, the expansion was related directly to the production of railroad equipment, which began in the 1870s. The good fortunes that this branch of industry experienced can be credited to some extent to its supply of entrepreneurs. Such men as Breda, Agnelli, and Olivetti traveled widely in Europe and the United States and introduced the most modern equipment and business techniques in Italy. Also, northern Italy had equipped itself with technical education facilities, the Politecnico of Turin (dating from 1859) and the Politecnico of Milan (dating from 1863), which were capable of training an indigenous workforce of technicians.

With industrial development so extensive in northern Italy, why was it necessary for such a large number of potential industrial workers to leave the country in order to find work? No definitive answer can be given to this question. However, as will be shown, it was not always necessity that pushed northern Italians to migrate to Switzerland. The Italian government chose to encourage emigration instead of choosing the alternative course of action, namely, channeling the manpower into Italian industry.

The third category of worker to leave northern Italy to work in Switzerland consisted of young Italian females. During the first decade of the twentieth century especially, there was a substantial increase in the number of Italian women working in Swiss industry.[84] They worked for the most part in the textile industry but also in chocolate- and tobacco-processing factories, restaurants and hotels, and clothing production.

When analyzing this group's motivations for emigrating, the evidence for an economic push out of the homeland is similarly unconvincing. During the same period, for instance, prospects for female employment in northern Italy were increasing rapidly. According to Hunecke's description of burgeoning industrialization in Milan after 1890, female factory workers formed an important part of the labor force. Many of Milan's large firms, such as Binda's button factory, De Angeli's dye works, and Pirelli's rubber factory, employed a large percentage of female workers. In fact, female employment was an intrinsic part of the modernization process. The new work force, *gente nuova*, which came from either the suburbs surrounding Milan or the countryside (for example, Pirelli's immigrants from the plains), consisted of two-thirds women and children. They were "fresh from the countryside, still unused to urban needs and malleable enough to be subjected to the new organization of work and production."[85]

In the textile industry in northern Italy, in particular, Italian women were experiencing increased employment prospects. The woolen centers in Piedmont and the cotton spinning mills around Milan, the silk mills around Como in Lombardy and around Mondovi in Piedmont were well-established and prospering industrial landmarks by this period. Women had largely replaced the formerly male work force in the textile industry in Milan by the last quarter of the nineteenth century. By 1901, 70 percent of the work force were female.[86]

In addition to female employment in factories, there was also a growing number of jobs in clothing production. This work, which was 84 percent female,[87] was performed in the woman's own home under conditions proverbially described as the *Elend der Schwitzarbeiter* (the misery of the sweatshop).

However, it was primarily to Swiss textile factories and clothing-production centers that Italian women migrated. How can the population movement be explained when Italian industry was flourishing and providing expanding job opportunities? It is the contention here that the Italian government at the beginning of the twentieth century encouraged the emigration of working females as well as other potential workers considered to be superfluous.

ITALIAN GOVERNMENT AND EMIGRATION

According to Foerster, the Italian government assumed various attitudes about emigration during the period between unification and the outbreak of World War I. Until the administration of Francesco Crispi in 1887, the government as well as the writers of the time considered emigration to be "a very grave evil for the country."[88]

When Crispi came to power, however, the attitude of the government became less clear-cut. In a recent article by Enrico Serra, dealing specifically with emigration to France during Crispi's first administration, emigration policies were described as follows:

> Crispi's policy on emigration was certainly more energetic than that of his predecessors. But, as Manzotti has rightly observed, it was also hesitant and contradictory, shifting between recognition of the loss of manpower involved, on one hand, and the undoubted economic and social advantages on the other.[89]

At any rate, Crispi was responsible for the first Italian legislation on emigration, the emigration act of May 1888, which tried to impose governmental regulation and curtail abusive activities of transportation companies involved in emigration by sea. The major significance of the law, in retrospect, may have been the establishment of the principle that the government had a role to play in the matter of emigration. In fact, the law's purpose was to attempt to restrict emigration while at the same time safeguarding the emigrants' interests.

Between 1891, when Crispi's first administration ended, and 1908, Foerster suggests that the Italian government's attitude regarding emigration changed.[90] During this period, the advantages to Italy of emigration were emphasized. The emigration law of 1901 set up a governmental office in Rome to organize and control the flow of emigration, which until then had been "planless, chaotic and uncontrolled."[91] The head of the office, the commissioner-general of emigration, had wide-ranging responsibilities including protection of emigrants' health; licensing emigrant carriers; publishing an information bulletin; and appropriating money for exhibitions, hospitals, welfare organizations, and employment bureaus in the countries of immigration. "In 1905, the Commissioner-General . . . appointed two emigration attaches for the industrial region in West Germany, and one for Switzerland. These . . . give their entire time to watching over and helping the emigrants—studying the labor market, visiting workplaces, advising when there are strikes, helping to secure accident indemnities."[92] With the enactment of this law, it can be seen that the Italian government not only recognized the existence of Italian emigration but also attempted to assist the emigrant.

During the period between 1908 and World War I, Foerster described governmental policies as encouraging emigration. There was a connection between official attitudes concerning emigration and imperialism. If emigration could be directed to those countries that Italy had colonized, then the expanding empire could provide an outlet for excess population. The Italian empire encouraged emigration to Somaliland (annexed in 1889), Eritrea (annexed in 1890), and Libya (annexed in 1911). A movement of writers and politicians known as the Nationalists, who emerged in the early twentieth century, gave theoretical underpinnings to governmental policies. Enrico Corradini, founder of the movement, wrote, "Emigration is one of the points of departure of Nationalism, one of the very determiners of its character."[93] Furthermore, "emigration signifies the abandonment of Italian labor to itself throughout the world, whereas conquest of colonies signifies Italian labor accompanied through the world by other forces of the Italian nation, by the nation itself."[94] Imperialist intentions also extended to Switzerland. Ticino, the Italian-speaking southern Swiss canton, was openly discussed as a possible region for the extension of the Italian mainland.[95]

What explanation can be found for the Italian governments' change of attitude regarding emigration? Why did the government discourage Italian emigration during the midnineteenth century, attempt to assist it in the late nineteenth century, then try to expand it at the beginning of the twentieth century? Three reasons may be suggested. Since unification in 1861, Italy had a continual trade deficit, which became positive only during the year 1871 and the Second World War. The government was, therefore, always seeking solutions to balance of payments problems, and emigrant remittances were one solution. Considerable funds flowed into Italy during the years of heaviest emigration preceding World War I. During the financial crisis of 1907, when Italy was cut off from French loans, emigrant remittances are reputed to have dampened the impact of the crisis by providing an alternative supply of capital.[96]

In economies where population increases faster than the labor market, it has been acknowledged economic wisdom that two policy options are available to a government: Either increase the product or reduce the population.[97] The Italian government before World War I took the second option, to reduce the population, by encouraging emigration. However, Moore described some of the disadvantages of the policy: "It may have made possible the continuance of high reproductive rates."[98] Furthermore, although remittances contributed somewhat to the well-being of those left behind, "savings were used not only to pay off farm indebtedness but also to bid up land prices to uneconomic levels."[99]

Furthermore, the Italian government's interest in encouraging emigration may have been the result of external pressures. Webster has shown that foreign capitalists exerted considerable influence on the Italian economy, especially during the period of rapid industrialization, from 1890 to 1907.[100] His description of the investment program of the Banca Commerciale of Milan during the period illustrates how foreign influence could have affected the Italian government's economic decision making. The bank, whose funds came from German, Swiss, French, and Italian shareholders, had mainly foreign directors.[101] "The bank's foreign associates and stockholder representatives objected vigorously to the Commerciale's tying up capital in long-term domestic industrial credit."[102] Rather, "its foreign backers kept insisting on liquidity, on assets that could be turned into fast cash for emergencies, and on diversification of the bank's credit risks."[103] The Italian economy depended heavily on foreign capital and such banks as Banca Commerciale. The Italian government was not in a position to decide independently to invest in Italian industrial development. It is understandable, therefore, that the Italian government opted to encourage emigration when faced with the two factors of foreign discouragement of investments in Italian industry and the immediate benefits to be gained from emigrant remittances.

Another possible explanation for the Italian government's encouragement of emigration may have been related to the continual efforts to eliminate political opposition. Emigration could be regarded as an instrument in the campaign to rid the country of troublesome elements. Emigration from northern Italy might have been especially significant, for this region was closely associated with the growth of the Socialist party and the trade union movement. During the 1890s, when migration to Switzerland was growing rapidly, the Italian government attempted continually to block the spread of socialism. According to Horowitz, northern Italy and in particular Lombardy were at the very center of the socialist movement. At the inauguration of the Socialist party in 1892, the Lombardy group was "the dominant element," and in local elections in Milan, Bergamo, Cremona, and Pavia, socialists received wide support.[104]

The national government's resistance to this political movement was determined. Several efforts to block electoral successes throughout the 1890s culminated in 1898 in the arrest of most Socialist party leaders after the so-called "tragedy of Milan" in 6–9 May. A strike at the Pirelli factory led to "a truly revolutionary situation," as James Joll described, "with the erection of barricades and open hostilities between demonstrators and the army."[105] The death toll amounted to 80, with 450 injured.

One Italian immigrant, who was only fourteen when he left to work on a seasonal contract in Switzerland in 1899, reported that "the repression of the Milan riot led to a strong wave of political emigration."[106] A future Italian political leader, Rinaldo Rigola of the woolen textile town of Biella in northern Italy, had been forced to flee from Italy at this time. "After a short stay in Switzerland, he settled in Lyon," from where he was elected to the Italian parliament while still in exile in 1900.[107] Even

Mussolini is said to have lived in Switzerland for a short time during this period.[108]

It was not only political activists who emigrated, but people involved in any of the various trade union associations. Even though "until 1889 trade unions were virtually forbidden and the strike . . . was illegal unless the workers could show reasonable cause," nonetheless there were continual attempts to establish unions of one sort or another during this period.[109] Early trade-union-type societies were to be found among printers, railroad builders, and farm laborers. The number of strikes among both industrial and agricultural workers rose measurably during the prewar period: In 1901 and again in 1907, several hundred thousand workers took part in strike action.[110] Female workers in the textile industry in northern Italy also participated in trade union activity, mainly in the Catholic trade unions, which were the least militant organizations. These unions "rejected class struggles in favor of collaboration and cooperation . . . [and] recognized strikes as a legitimate last resort in labor disputes."[111] Catholic trade unions relied on women for 35.9 percent of the 104,600 membership in 1910.[112]

The Italian government that encouraged working-age males as well as females to leave northern Italy to work in Switzerland could be seen to have been responding to a wide range of economic and political pressures. The Italians who emigrated, however, were also responding to several factors: On the one hand, they were pushed out of Italy, but on the other, they were attracted by expanding economic opportunities in Switzerland.

4

EMPLOYMENT OF FOREIGNERS IN SWISS MANUFACTURING

The manufacturing industries of Switzerland during the period from 1888 to 1914 exerted a strong pull on populations in countries to the north and south. In Chapter 3, internal conditions in southern Germany and northern Italy that motivated emigration were analyzed. Here and in chapters 5–7, attractions of the Swiss economy to migrants are described.

The secondary sector of the Swiss economy employed the largest proportion of foreign workers. More than 60 percent of the nearly 300,000 foreign workers in Switzerland in 1910 worked in the secondary sector.[1] This chapter presents an overview of the impact made by foreigners on the growth of Swiss manufacturing industries. The history of eight industries are summarized.

Swiss historians have often mentioned that foreign workers helped satisfy the demand for labor in Switzerland during the quarter century preceding World War I. Bickel wrote that "the economic upswing at the end of the nineteenth century would have been impossible without immigration, because without it there would have been a very severe shortage of workers (including also the shortage of certain skilled occupations)."[2] However, few Swiss historians have analyzed the types of effects foreign workers had on the growth of manufacturing.

In this study, two major roles that foreigners performed in Swiss manufacturing industries have been identified. By examining the data, it was found that foreign workers performed similar functions in more than one branch of manufacturing. The main functions have been formulated into two roles—each is a broadly defined category, more applicable to some branches than to others. Since foreigners were employed in a variety of jobs in a wide range of industries, it has not been possible to include all the specific roles performed in the two categories. The roles, therefore, are generalized descriptions of the impact of foreigners on Swiss manufacturing industries.

Role 1: Foreign workers attracted to Swiss industry provided the labor force necessary for introducing mass production methods of manufacture. That is, foreign labor enabled Swiss industries to change from hand production in workshops or cottages to machine production in factories.

Foreigners, who increasingly originated from Italy, were employed in factories to manufacture with machinery products that previously had been hand produced. They either supplemented the indigenous work force or replaced Swiss workers.

With the new manufacturing system, output rose as documented in export statistics. The change was most evident in the textile, metalworking, shoe, and building materials industries.

Foreign labor also enabled the establishment of new, factory-based branches of manufacture.

Several new branches of industry were founded during the prewar period. The new industries recruited workers among the Swiss population and also in neighboring countries. Foreign workers were important components of the work force in aluminum, electrical engineering, chemical, and some types of processed foods manufacture.

Role 2: Foreign workers attracted to Swiss industry provided one linkage in the interdependent industrial development of central European economic regions. The free migration of labor between countries in central Europe was part and parcel of an entire range of economic connections. The Swiss economy was most closely associated with the German economy during the prewar period. In several branches of industry, technology was exchanged, trade was expanded, capital was transferred, and trade union strategies were coordinated. In some branches of industry, regional economic connections existed with France, Italy, and Austria-Hungary. None of the connections, however, was so extensive as the German-Swiss one, which was especially important to the growth of the engineering, chemical, food-processing, and printing industries.

Foreign workers were attracted to Swiss industry because of the comparatively slower pace of industrial modernization in Switzerland. During the prewar period, the contrast in industrialization was mainly between the Swiss and German economies. German skilled workers, such as carpenters, mechanics, foundrymen, tailors, brewers, and printers, migrated to Switzerland to practice a trade in a more traditional environment. The link between the two economies could be described as complementary. Rapidly industrializing Germany had an outlet for structurally unemployed artisans in less rapidly industrializing Switzerland. In several manufacturing branches, the migration of skilled German labor to Switzerland was not new, but a continuation of traditions maintained throughout the nineteenth century.

In 1888, the factory system of production was not yet widespread throughout Swiss manufacturing industries. The cottage system and artisan production continued to be important methods of manufacture. Kneschaurek calculated that 33 percent of employment in Swiss industry in 1888 took place in factories;[3] by 1910, it had increased to approximately 47 percent.[4] The definition of a Swiss factory, however, was a very broad one: "Included as factories were all industrial establishments which employed eleven or more persons, or if the firm used motorized machinery it needed to employ only six persons or more to be designated a factory. Also included were establishments in which there was unusual danger to the life and health of the worker regardless of size of workforce."[5]

Using employment data compiled from the Swiss census of 1910 and from the federal factory statistics of 1911, it has been possible to divide the industrial branches according to the extent of factory penetration of production. In clothing, food-processing and wood-processing industries, more than half the work force was still employed in the cottage system or workshop in 1910. On the other hand, engineering, chemicals, and the manufacture of building materials were factory-based industries by this time. Watchmaking, printing, metalworking, and textile manufacture were partly factory based and partly workshop or cottage based. In all manufacturing industries, foreigners were increasingly employed in factory manufacture. Whereas in 1900, 48 percent of the foreigners employed in Swiss industry worked in factories, by 1910, the figure had risen to 61 percent.[6] Not only did the number of foreigners in Swiss factories increase significantly, but the country of origin of foreign factory workers changed as well. In 1894 and 1901, foreigners originating from Germany were the most numerous; by 1911, however, foreigners from Italy predominated.[7]

The considerable growth of Italian factory workers in Switzerland led contemporary commentators to compare them to foreign workers in other countries, who acted as "a second rate workforce" (*Arbeiterschicht zweiten Grades*). "The Italians in Switzerland are like the Negro in the United States, the Chinese in California, the east Indian coolie in the British West Indies, the Japanese in Hawaii, the Polynesian in Australia."[8]

Foreign factory workers were naturally attracted to the cantons in Switzerland that were rapidly industrializing, such as Zurich, St. Gall, and Thurgau. Nonetheless, there is another locational pattern discernible in the geography of foreign workers in Swiss factories in 1911. Nationals of Germany, Italy, and France tended to work in cantons closest to their own countries.

For example, German factory workers were most numerous in Zurich,

Basel-Town, St. Gall, Thurgau, and Schaffhausen.[9] These cantons are located in the north of Switzerland, near the borders of Baden or Württemberg; motives for the migration from southern Germany are discussed in Chapter 3. Here, it is important to underline the attraction that Swiss industries exerted on southern Germans. However, the pull to Switzerland was not powerful enough to encourage Germans to migrate in sizable numbers to factories in south, west, or central Switzerland. Therefore, the close connections between the German-speaking north of Switzerland and south Germany must be taken into consideration in analyzing the population movement. Not only push and pull factors, but also more intangible social and economic ties that traditionally drew the regions together are factors of considerable importance in understanding why southern Germans worked in Swiss factories before World War I.

Similarly, French factory workers in Switzerland tended to migrate mainly to the canton of Geneva.[10] Italian factory workers were more widely dispersed throughout Switzerland, although a large number remained in the neighboring canton, Ticino.[11]

Foreigners worked in Swiss manufacturing industries mainly as laborers. In 1910, 80 percent of all foreign workers were either skilled or unskilled workers.[12] When the employment status of foreigners was compared with the employment status of the Swiss working population, considerable differences were apparent.[13] Even though more than 60 percent of the Swiss were employed as laborers, approximately 30 percent operated their own manufacturing businesses. Furthermore, the Swiss were not widely employed as unskilled laborers. Unskilled work, which consisted of a variety of undesired jobs, such as carrying, cleaning, or assisting skilled workmen, was left to foreign workers.

Foreigners did not normally compete with the Swiss for jobs. Some branches of manufacturing had become accessible to foreigners by the nineteenth century. Some types of skilled work in printing, wood processing, engineering, clothing manufacture, building materials, and food processing were often the preserve of foreigners. They usually worked alongside the Swiss population and did not control any of the manufacturing branches. The role of German foreign workers in these occupations became part of Swiss tradition (role 2).

By the end of the nineteenth century, Switzerland's expanding manufacturing industries demanded more factory workers. The limited Swiss population was not sufficient; foreigners, therefore, were employed to fill the void. In some cantons, however, Swiss women provided some of the additional factory labor, especially in watchmaking, food processing, printing, and shoe making. Swiss factory legislation had restricted the employment of children, and much of the Swiss rural

population had emigrated overseas rather than work in factories.[14] Foreigners were employed as a supplementary factory work force in the
chemical, textile, and building materials industries and to a lesser extent
in engineering, metalworking, wood processing, shoes, food processing, printing, and watchmaking (role 1).

Textiles

The Swiss manufacturing industry that employed the largest number
of foreign workers was the textile industry. According to the Swiss
census of 1910, nearly twenty-seven thousand foreigners worked in the
Swiss textile industry, comprising 15 percent of the work force.[15]

As workers in cotton and silk factories, they supplemented and partly
replaced the traditional domestic work force. With a supply of cheap
foreign labor, Swiss textile manufacturers were able to modernize factories and competitively mass produce textiles for export well into the
twentieth century (role 1).

In the embroidery branch of the textile industry, foreign workers were
introduced along with automatic embroidery machines. They were part
of the transformation process of Swiss embroideries from a domestic
handicraft into a large-scale export industry. Chapter 5 analyzes the role
of foreigners in this manufacturing industry.

Clothing and Shoes

The number of foreigners employed in this manufacturing branch was
only slightly fewer than in textile manufacture.[16] In 1910, 24,044 foreigners, half of whom were women, worked in clothing and shoe manufacture, accounting for 20 percent of the work force.[17] Clothing
manufacture, unlike textile production, was still largely a non-factory-
based industry before World War I. Factory-manufactured clothing experienced a slow start in Switzerland. Some have credited this to the
resistance of the domestic market to mass-produced articles of clothing.
As recently as the 1950s, it was reported that Swiss women commonly
made a large proportion of the family's clothing and did not buy ready-
made clothing to the same extent as in other industrialized countries.[18]

In 1888, only five factories, employing a total of three hundred people,
produced ready-made garments in Switzerland.[19] By 1911, only 20 percent of those employed in the manufacture of clothing and shoes worked
in a factory.[20] Garment manufacture took place in either a small urban
workshop or a worker's home as part of the domestic system of production.

According to Steiger, conditions in clothing workshops during the quarter century before World War I were especially bad. Women worked very long hours: A twelve-hour day was average, but during the height of the season, most clothing workers spent eighteen hours and Sundays at the workshop. In 1894, legislation in Zurich (Female Workers' Protection Law, or *Arbeiterinnenschutzgesetz*) was enacted, which was intended to reduce the daily working day to ten hours and nine hours on weekends and to forbid overtime work for girls under eighteen. However, not until 1906 was an inspector appointed to oversee compliance with the regulations.[21] During the summer of 1913, the Confederation of Swiss Women's Associations *(Der Bund Schweizerischer Frauenvereine)* concluded that women working in the clothing industry were still overworked and underpaid. According to findings of the report, seamstresses and milliners normally worked a ten-hour day, but people employed to iron worked longer hours. During high season, one-quarter of the total employed worked a twelve-hour day. Earnings rarely reached one hundred Swiss francs per month.[22]

In the cottage production of clothing, conditions were even worse. At the Swiss Cottage Industry Exhibition *(Schweizerischen Heimarbeitsausstellung)*, which was held in Zurich in 1909, normal rates paid for sewing items of clothing were listed.[23] Since the cottage worker paid for raw materials, equipment, light, heat, and rent, earnings were seldom adequate to cover living expenses.

Foreign women who accompanied their husbands to Switzerland fit into a pattern of marginal employment in the Swiss clothing industry.[24] They had relatively easy access into small workshops or the cottage industry because of the long-established position of foreign tailors in Switzerland.

Foreign men played a different role from foreign women in the Swiss clothing industry. In several Swiss cities, they were employers, operators of small workshops. The garment industry was the only manufacturing branch in Switzerland in which a sizable number of foreign workers was self-employed in 1910.[25] The German tailor was a familiar sight in Swiss cities until World War I. In Zurich, approximately half the men's tailors was foreign born in 1910; in Basel, more than 60 percent and in St. Gall, nearly 50 percent.[26] Germans were not the only foreign tailors who worked in Switzerland, for there were French tailors in Geneva and Italian tailors in Ticino.[27]

The traditional presence of foreigners in the Swiss clothing industry and the functions they performed in the Swiss economy fit into what has been identified as role 2—foreigners were part of the interdependent industrialization of Germany and Switzerland. Throughout the nineteenth century, German tailors were one of the principal types of skilled worker participating in what Gruner has called "the proverbial wandering" *(sprichwörtliche Wanderlust).*[28] Foreign tailors in Switzerland were instrumental in developing trade unions in the midnineteenth century. Local branches of tailor and shoemaker trade unions were among the earliest established unions in Switzerland. Germans were important in the formative years. Some Swiss scholars contend that Swiss unions were modeled on German working men's associations *(Handwerkervereine).*[29]

As previously described, the Swiss garment industry in the nineteenth century consisted of small-scale undertakings and catered to individual demand. The foreign tailor in Switzerland was part of an European division of labor. He continued manufacturing clothing of high quality in Switzerland, whereas in Paris, Berlin, and Vienna, large-scale clothing manufacturers developed cottage and factory production of inexpensive, basic clothing.[30] During the prewar period, a major portion of linens and underclothing sold in Switzerland was imported from Germany and Paris.[31] Switzerland was a logical destination for skilled tailors and seamstresses,[32] because the traditional Swiss garment trade was more accessible to artisans than the large, competitive industry in Germany.

In the manufacture of shoes, the transition to factory production was not so retarded in Switzerland. Carl Franz Bally, whose family origins have been traced to the Austrian Vorarlberg,[33] began manufacturing machine-made shoes in Schönenewerd in canton Solothurn in 1854. In order to operate the factory, "which produced hand-made shoes on old type weaving machines,"[34] he recruited skilled technicians from France and Germany. The company's shoes, however, were largely exported, for the indigenous population mistrusted factory-made shoes.[35] By the 1870s, Bally had established subsidiaries in several foreign countries as far afield as South America.

The example provided by Bally was copied by other entrepreneurs in the late nineteenth century. Between 1888 and 1895, twenty shoe factories were set up in Switzerland.[36] In comparison with other Swiss industries, shoe factories were large-scale operations. Lehmann found that an average-sized shoe factory employed 129 workers in 1895.[37]

In contrast to clothing production, the shoe industry employed an equal and large number of both Germans and Italians.[38] In 1910, foreigners comprised 24 percent of the total work force.[39] Foreigners who worked in the Swiss shoe industry were predominantly male, whereas the clothing industry included a large number of female foreign workers.

Foreigners in the industry were employed throughout Switzerland, with large concentrations only in Zurich and Thurgau.[40] However, in the cantons of Solothurn and Aargau, where the largest number of shoe workers was to be found, foreigners represented an insignificant portion of the work force. In these two cantons, on the other hand, the number of Swiss women employed in shoe manufacture was substantial.[41]

With the introduction of machinery, which had the effect of deskilling the shoe-manufacturing process, a new work force was required. In cantons where female labor had been underemployed, Swiss women could be trained for this type of employment. One of the earliest employers of female labor in the shoe industry was Kaspar Appenzeller, who set up an industrial educational institution for women in Tagelswangen (canton Zurich) in 1874.[42] Women were employed in shoe factories especially for sewing, stamping, polishing, and fastening straps on shoes. Male labor was required for preparing the leather and operating heavy equipment.

Foreign men and Swiss women together performed role 1 in the Swiss shoe industry, for they enabled the industry to introduce mass production processes before World War I. An expanding industry in demand of additional workers used both foreign and female labor.

Foreigners also performed role 2: They formed one link in the interdependent industrial development of Germany and Switzerland, especially in Swiss cities where they perpetuated the artisan's manufacture of shoes. Both German shoemakers and German tailors were prevalent in Switzerland during the nineteenth century. The German shoemaker established trade union links between the two countries, introduced production techniques and shoe styles into Switzerland from Germany, and helped maintain trade, especially the import of leather from Germany. Although factory production was rapidly replacing craft production of shoes during the prewar period, nonetheless, the self-employed foreign shoemaker continued to repair and make a limited quantity of handmade shoes. Not all shoemakers were from Germany, for Italians also worked as self-employed shoemakers in Switzerland, primarily in Geneva.

Food Processing

Foreign workers performed both roles 1 and 2 in the Swiss food-processing industry. In the new factories that produced canned foods, tobacco, chocolate, and soft drinks, foreigners contributed significantly to the labor supply, enabling the industry to introduce mass production processes (role 1). At the same time, the traditional presence of skilled Germans who worked as butchers, bakers, and beer brewers, as well as innovating entrepreneurs helped maintain strong links between the industries of Germany and Switzerland (role 2).

It is somewhat ironic that the food-processing industry, which has been described as "the most national of Swiss industries,"[43] employed an increasing number of foreigners during the early twentieth century. In 1910, 19 percent of those employed in this industry were foreign.[44] Foreign workers participated, however, in some branches of food processing to a greater extent than in others. Agricultural-related production, such as the manufacture of cheese and milk, in which foreigners did not work, was in fact more part of the primary sector of the economy than the secondary sector. Swiss mountain farmers had long organized the production of dairy products and did not employ foreign workers.

The food-processing industry as a whole was only partly factory based at the outbreak of World War I. Thirty-eight percent of those employed in the industry in 1911 worked in a factory.[45] Foreign workers were employed in both factory and nonfactory branches of food processing. Italians tended to work in factories, whereas Germans continued to work as butchers, bakers, and beer brewers in more traditionally operated branches of the industry.

Until the first decade of the twentieth century, foreigners working in the food-processing industry in Switzerland came primarily from Germany. Germans dominated the Swiss beer-brewing business, especially in Zurich, Bern, Basel, St. Gall, and Aargau. Furthermore, many of the pioneering entrepreneurs were immigrants from Germany.

Heinrich Nestlé, the inventor of baby cereal and founder of the food company that bears his name, was born in Frankfurt am Main in 1814. He migrated to Switzerland and became a salesman of mustard, seeds, and petroleum lamps in Vevey on Lake Geneva in 1843. He maintained business contacts with his German homeland, for in 1868, he was selling his baby food in both Vevey and Frankfurt.[46] Karl Albert Wander, of Dr. A Wander AG, Bern, the inventor of ovomaltine in 1904, was the son of a German immigrant.[47] Gustav Henckell founded the jam-manufacturing company Hero Conserven Lenzbourg in 1885 with another German immigrant.[48]

Skilled workers and entrepreneurs from Germany performed role 2 in the Swiss food-processing industry by promoting strong links between the industries of Switzerland and Germany. New technology and manufacturing processes were introduced in Switzerland through immigrants. Furthermore, as previously enumerated, several food products would not have been manufactured in Switzerland without the inventions of German immigrants who were a channel for inflows of capital into Swiss food-processing businesses as well as a channel for imports and exports to and from Germany.

But by 1911, the number of Italians working in Swiss food-processing factories exceeded the number of Germans.[49] In fact, the new factory work force consisted in large measure of foreign women, who were more prevalent than foreign men in chocolate factories, fruit and vegetable preservation, and soup factories.

Foreign factory workers performed role 1 in the Swiss food-processing industry. They enabled the industry to introduce mass production techniques and start the manufacture of new products. Although in some types of food-processing factories, Swiss women provided most of the labor,[50] foreign workers still represented a substantial proportion of the factory work force throughout the industry.

In the manufacture of chocolate, for example, foreigners comprised 19 percent of the work force, with foreign women somewhat more numerous than foreign men in 1910.[51] The beginnings of chocolate manufacture in Switzerland belong to an earlier period of history. F. L. Cailler's invention in 1819 led to the establishment during the course of the nineteenth century of other still famous companies, such as Suchard (1826), Kohler (1830), Sprüngli (1845), Klaus (1856), Peter (1867), Tobler (1869), Lindt (1879), and Nestlé (started to manufacture chocolate in 1904).[52] The nineteenth-century chocolate industry was located mainly in French-speaking Switzerland, especially in the cantons of Vaud, Neuchâtel, and Fribourg.

During the prewar period, when foreigners became a sizable part of the work force, chocolate production became large scale and export expansive. The value of chocolate exports rose from 1,944,000 Swiss francs in 1886 to 55,232,000 Swiss francs in 1912.[53] Earlier established family firms were converted into limited companies in the late nineteenth century. New factories were constructed, and in the early twentieth century, several producers associations were formed.[54]

The expanding chocolate industry required an additional supply of labor. In the case of one company, Cailler, the work force increased from 120 workers in 1898 to 1,373 workers in 1905.[55] Foreign workers contributed significantly to the labor supply. "On one occasion at least, the Cailler company brought two hundred Italian girls to Fribourg, enrolled by an agent at Pavullo [in Emilia Romagna, Italy], with the approval of Italian officials."[56] According to a contemporary writer, the Italian girls brought to work in large Swiss chocolate factories were between the ages of fourteen and twenty. Their daily wages varied between 1.50 and 2.50 Swiss francs for a ten-hour working day.[57]

Chocolate manufacturing during the period also spread beyond the confines of French-speaking Switzerland. In two cantons in particular, Lucerne and Ticino, where chocolate was still produced on a limited scale, foreign workers provided the majority of the work force.[58]

It can be seen that foreign workers performed an important role in the growth of Swiss chocolate production. By examining another branch of the food-processing industry more closely, the role of foreigners may be further elucidated.

Tobacco, though not strictly a food but similar enough to be always listed in the same category in Swiss statistics, provides a good example. Tobacco processing involved all the various and sometimes conflicting aspects of Swiss development in manufacturing. Tobacco was processed by means of both the domestic and the factory system, using hand methods and machinery and employing Swiss and foreign female labor.

In 1910, a total of 9,127 people was listed in the Swiss census as employed in tobacco processing. Although this was not a large number for Swiss manufacturing employment as a whole, nevertheless for the cantons of Aargau, Vaud, and Ticino, where the workers were mainly to be found, it was of some significance.[59] For example, in the 1860s when the Aargau cigar industry expanded, jobs in the industry offered a welcome income to otherwise unemployed hand weavers.[60]

Even though agricultural conditions in Switzerland were not ideal for cultivating tobacco, there was indigenous production in those three cantons. In the canton of Vaud, near Lake Neuchâtel in the valley of the river Broye, the largest expanses of tobacco cultivation in Switzerland were located. In the canton of Ticino, tobacco was grown as part of a system known as *Doppelkulturen*, (double cultivation), which involved planting tobacco on small parcels of land usually between rows of grapes.

Swiss tobacco processing made use of two methods of production during this period. In canton Aargau, processing was organized as a cottage industry, with hand laborers making cigars at home. In Ticino, on the other hand, factories that employed more than one hundred workers were already in existence in 1870.[61]

The labor force in the industry was primarily female. According to the 1910 census, nearly twice as many women as men were employed in Swiss tobacco processing.[62] Light industrial work, which involved finger dexterity, such as rolling and wrapping cigars, had become, since the midnineteenth century, the preserve of female workers.

The growth of the Swiss tobacco industry into a factory-operated, mainly female industry led to its importance as an employer of foreign workers during the first decade of the twentieth century. Twenty percent of the work force were foreign in 1910, and the majority of the workers consisted of Italian women.

A closer examination of the census reveals additional information about how foreign workers were deployed. Even though the canton of Aargau had the largest total tobacco-processing work force, foreigners were not most numerous there. Instead, the cantons of Vaud and Ticino employed more foreign workers.[63] This can be related directly to the method of production used in each canton. As previously described, machine production in factories was the mode of operation in Vaud and Ticino, whereas in Aargau, tobacco manufacturing remained a cottage industry. Foreigners could be employed advantageously in factory production, and their availability enabled the expansion of mass production in the Swiss tobacco industry (role 1).

Chemicals

The Swiss chemical industry provides an example of both types of roles that foreigners performed in Swiss manufacturing. In 1910, foreign workers from Germany and Italy comprised 22 percent of the work force,[64] enabling the introduction of mass production (role 1). At the same time chemical manufacture in Switzerland was closely related to developments in other European countries. Foreigners were one link in the interdependent development of the French and Swiss industries during the midnineteenth century. By the prewar period, foreign workers helped strengthen connections between chemical industries in Germany and Switzerland (role 2).

The first dyestuff factories in Basel were set up to service the cotton textile industry in neighboring Alsace. Mulhouse in Alsace has often been equated to Manchester in England, as an early center of French textile manufacture. Basel, only twenty miles away but in a different country with different legislation and resources, was in an ideal position to take advantage of Alsatian demand.

By the middle of the nineteenth century, not only were small Swiss chemical firms marketing dyes in Alsace, but they were also importing workers from this industrial region. According to Burckhardt, the historian of the city of Basel, Alsatians were employed in Switzerland at a lower salary than Swiss and could be sent back to their homeland when business conditions were depressed;[65] in addition, the city of Basel was not obligated to provide for their poor relief.

Highly skilled French chemists found opportunity in Basel. Both the Gesellschaft für Chemische Industrie Basel (CIBA) and Durand & Huguenin were established by Frenchmen in the midnineteenth century. Alexander Clavel from Lyon started CIBA in 1859, and Jean Gaspard Dollfuss of Mulhouse began to manufacture synthetic dyestuffs in Basel in 1862. Dullfuss's firm was the forerunner of the present firm, Durand & Huguenin. Another French chemist, Armand Gerber, also from Mulhouse, set up an aniline dye factory in Basel in 1864. He had come to Switzerland to escape from the French patent law. He had been fined in France for producing a dyestuff called azaleine, which he had discovered. The French court, however, had decided that azaleine was chemically identical to the already existing dye fuchsine, and the court therefore banned production of the former in France.[66]

Connections between the Swiss and German chemical industries developed somewhat later than the Franco-Swiss connection. Nonetheless, with regard to market division, scientific collaboration, and the migration of labor, links between the chemical industries of Germany and Switzerland were more extensive.

During the quarter century preceding World War I, the Swiss chemical industry was still in its infancy. The present five chemical giants, CIBA, Hoffmann-LaRoche, Geigy, Sandoz, and Durand & Huguenin had been established, but only CIBA employed a work force of more than one thousand. Exports were still insignificant.[67] Swiss chemical factories were almost all located in Basel or in the extreme south of the country, in the mountainous canton of Valais. In the Rhone Valley (Valais), an electrochemical industry was established, using newly available hydroelectric power. The Basle Chemische Fabriken, which was taken over by CIBA in 1908, was the major industrial employer in lower Valais during the prewar period. Lonza AG, which had been founded in 1897 by Basel financiers, was the largest employer in upper Valais.

German factory workers were an important component of the factory work force. By 1901, one-fifth of the total work force in the Swiss chemical industry came from Germany. As in other Swiss industries, however, foreign factory workers from Italy were more numerous than those from Germany a decade later.[68] Swiss chemical manufacture was factory based by this period, and foreign workers provided a necessary part of the labor.

In addition to their role as part of the factory work force, Germans also made a significant contribution by transferring technology between the chemical industries of Germany and Switzerland. Scientists from the two countries collaborated on research and also moved freely from one country to another for training. During the late nineteenth century, scientists from CIBA and the German company Badische Anilin und Sodafabrik AG (BASF) jointly developed a new group of Rhodamine dyes.[69] The same German chemical company also manufactured a new synthetic indigo dye that Karl Heumann, a professor at the Swiss Federal Institute of Technology, had developed.[70] Alfred Kern, one of the co-founders of the present firm Sandoz Ltd., worked in an aniline factory in Offenbach am Main in Germany before founding the Basel dyestuffs factory in 1886 with Edouard Sandoz.[71] Munich-born and educated Max Carl Traub, who was the first partner in the firm of Hoffmann-LaRoche, decided to settle in Switzerland rather than his native Germany after qualifying as a chemist in Freiburg.[72]

The Swiss chemical industry developed very much in the shadow of its larger, northern neighbor and was dependent on Germany for raw materials, intermediates, and process chemicals. However, from the beginning, the manufacturers had worked out a relationship advantageous to both countries' industries. Switzerland produced several specialized products that Germany did not, such as high quality dyestuffs, and relied on Germany for the import of bulk dyestuffs and inorganic chemicals.[73]

The two chemical industries were also connected by the early growth of Swiss subsidiaries in Germany. Basel chemical firms set up several factories in Baden in southern Germany before World War I. Geigy started production in Grenzach, and CIBA also established a number of subsidiaries outside of Switzerland by this time. Fritz Hoffmann, founder of the pharmaceutical company Hoffmann-LaRoche, had originally looked for a factory site on the German side of the Rhine River in 1894 when starting production. Since German law accorded patent protection to imports for only three years, Hoffmann considered it preferable to locate a factory in Germany rather than Switzerland in order to reach the German market. In point of fact, the company's first factory was set up in Basel, but another one in Grenzach, Germany, was established before World War I. According to an official company history, "The works in Grenzach represented the base for chemical production during the war."[74]

The mutual growth of the Swiss and German chemical industries was further strengthened by geography. The southern German, or Rhineland, chemical industry and the Swiss industry in Basel were located within one industrial region. Within the region, trade, capital, and labor moved relatively freely.

Wood Processing

Foreign workers played both roles in the Swiss wood-processing industry. By 1910, foreigners comprised 22 percent of the total work force in the industry.[75] As factory workers, they enabled the industry to shift gradually to mass production processes (role 1). At the same time, however, the traditional presence of Germans employed as journeyman carpenters and woodworking artisans continued into the twentieth century. They established bonds between the industries in Switzerland and Germany, which led to interdependent industrial development (role 2).

Wood processing in Switzerland has been a many-faceted industry. During the prewar period, it encompassed saw mills for processing timber; workshops and factories for manufacturing furniture, toys, brushes, barrels, parquet floors, and joinery; and art studios for wood sculpture. At the beginning of the twentieth century, a considerable part of the production was transferred from workshops to factories.[76] At the same time, the value of exports increased.[77] However, wood processing was not primarily an export industry; it mainly supplied the home market.

Switzerland's extensive reserves of forests provided raw materials for the industry. Nearly one-quarter of the land's surface was in woodland.[78] For centuries, woodcarving had been a traditional rural craft; during the nineteenth century, Brienz in the Berner Oberland became a well-known center for the art. A technical school was founded, and the oldest wood-carving firm in Switzerland, Ed. Binder & Co, was started in 1835. Exports of handcrafted wood carvings from Brienz, such as wooden bears, musical boxes, and match boxes, have enjoyed a worldwide reputation.

Male foreign workers were attracted to the Swiss wood-processing industry from Germany, Italy, and Austria. At the outbreak of World War I, a woodworker in Switzerland could earn between forty-eight and sixty rappen per hour,[79] and with factory production expanding, there was increased demand for laborers. During the first decade of the twentieth century, the number of foreign workers employed in the industry increased 20 percent.[80] The additional foreigners were engaged in new factories, in which Germans were most numerous but where Italians were also well represented.[81]

Foreigners were also found in workshops and artisan shops, and some were self-employed. The latter were mainly Germans, many of whom had been attracted to the relatively less industrialized wood-processing industry in Switzerland. Reinhard Rigling, son of a carpenter in Watterdingen, Germany, was an example of such a German immigrant. He came to Zurich in 1894 during his journeyman's travels (Wanderschaft) and remained in Switzerland. In 1895, he bought land in an outlying area of Oerlikon, Zurich, and established a small workshop. His wood-processing firm employed twenty workers at the beginning of World War I. Rigling became a Swiss citizen in 1910, and his children took over the firm when he died in 1948.[82]

Throughout the nineteenth century, German carpenters migrated to Switzerland under similar circumstances. Skilled German woodworkers performed role 2 in the Swiss wood-processing industry. They were one link in the interdependent industrialization of Germany and Switzerland. As skilled craftsmen were pushed out of Germany by rapid industrial changes, the wood-processing industry in Switzerland provided access to a traditional livelihood. In one sense, labor migration reinforced a division of labor between industries in the two countries. German wood processing became large scale and oriented toward mass production while the Swiss wood-processing industry changed less rapidly and continued to be organized on a smaller scale.

Printing

Although the Swiss printing industry was not a major industrial employer, foreign workers nonetheless comprised 23 percent of the total work force.[83] With the introduction of typesetting equipment toward the end of the nineteenth century, the Swiss industry demanded factory workers. Unskilled foreigners were increasingly employed in factories, enabling the industry to use mass production processes (role 1).

Skilled foreign workers, predominantly of German origin, also performed role 2. They participated in the interdependent development of German language publishing. Germans had traditionally been important in book publishing, photography, and newspaper printing in Switzerland. Swiss cities had attracted skilled German printers throughout the nineteenth century, and several had worked in political publishing in Switzerland.[84]

The early trade union movement, beginning with the Bern Society of Printers' Journeymen *(Berner Verein der Buchdruckergesellen)* in 1848 and the Swiss Typographer's Association *(Schweizerischer Typographenbund)* in 1858, was in close contact with German trade unionism. "One can see the connection with the appearance of trade unions at the same time in Germany."[85] According to Gruner, the Bern Society of Printers was inspired by the German National Book Printers Association *(Nationalbuchdruckerverein)*. They drafted the rules of their organization based on the German model;[86] specifically, membership requirements and the types of action envisaged were the same as in Germany. In similarity with German trade unions in the printing trade, Swiss printers' unions were open to both employers and workers and accordingly concentrated on nonrevolutionary tactics in order to improve working conditions.

Book publishing historically has been associated with the Swiss city of Basel, where as early as the sixteenth century famous printers developed outside the guild structure. Such historic names as Bonifacius Amerbach, Froben, Petri, Cratander, and Episcopius were well known for printing early literature as well as works of biology. Although publishing continued to exist in Basel, publishing companies were also established in other Swiss cities by 1910. German foreign workers represented a substantial part of the printing work force in most of the new centers.[87]

There was considerable variation in earnings for foreign printers in different regions of Switzerland.[88] In Ticino, a compositor in the city of Lugano earned only forty rappen an hour, whereas in the French-speaking region a compositors' normal wage was sixty-seven rappen an hour. In German-speaking Switzerland, sixty-one rappen an hour was the standard wage for a compositor.

Foreigners, attracted to the Swiss printing industry, were a direct link between German, French, and Italian language publishing and Swiss publishing. They served political as well as economic functions for foreign communities throughout Switzerland.[89]

Engineering

Foreigners performed both roles 1 and 2 in the Swiss engineering industry. German engineers had migrated to Swiss engineering firms throughout the nineteenth century. They had been important in transferring technology and the growth of trade unions in Switzerland. During the quarter century preceding World War I, foreign factory workers from both Germany and Italy enabled the Swiss engineering industry to introduce mass production processes nd substantially expand machinery exports (role 1).

As engineering became large scale and international in scope, connections between German and Swiss engineering firms intensified. Exchanges of capital and trade, as well as labor, linked the industries of the two countries, leading to interdependent industrialization (role 2). The foreign impact on the Swiss engineering industry is analyzed in detail in Chapter 6.

Metalworking

This industry developed in close association with the Swiss engineering industry and exhibited many of the same characteristics in regard to the role of foreign labor. The large, traditional role played by Germans, as well as the rapid increase in the number of Italian factory workers in the prewar period, are reminiscent of features of the engineering industry. However, metalworking, in contrast to engineering, was not primarily an export industry in Switzerland. The industry manufactured products demanded by engineering firms. In many cases, the same companies were active in both metalworking and engineering.[90] As machinery exports expanded during the prewar period, the output of metalworking firms expanded as well.[91] Furthermore, whereas engineering was mainly factory based by the outbreak of World War I, many metalworking businesses were still small-scale workshops.[92] Nonetheless, by 1911 two-thirds of the total number of foreigners employed in the Swiss metalworking industry worked in factories.[93] The three thousand additional foreigners employed during the first decade of the twentieth century represented a significant addition to the new factory work force. In this industry, foreign workers performed role 1 during the period, since they assisted in the transformation to factory production.

Metalworking in Switzerland consisted traditionally of iron and steel production, based on iron reserves mined in the Jura mountains. The first rolling mill was established in 1836, but by 1850, the Swiss iron industry had already contracted. Competition from inexpensive imported steel forced five of the six existent blast furnaces to stop production in the 1850s.

Nonetheless, there were other metals processed in Switzerland apart from iron. Such metals as copper, brass, nickel, and tin had long been processed at a number of small concerns in the German-speaking region of the country. At the end of the nineteenth century with exploitation of hydroelectricity, production of aluminum was a new addition to the metalworking industry.

Aluminum production was first undertaken in 1887 to 1888 in Neuhausen in the canton of Schaffhausen. The Rhine Falls, reputed to be the most powerful waterfall in Europe, provided the hydroelectric power. The firm, Aluminum AG, which today is called Alusuisse, moved production to the canton of Valais during the first decade of the twentieth century. The firm was the only Swiss producer of aluminum before World War I and therefore accounted solely for the considerable growth in exports. In 1892, the value of Swiss aluminum exports amounted to only 1.8 million Swiss francs but by 1912, had increased to 12.4 million Swiss francs.[94] In 1910, foreign workers comprised nearly half of the work force in the aluminum industry in Valais.[95]

Swiss historians have emphasized the importance of the mountain peasant whose work contributed to the growth of industry in the canton of Valais. During the quarter-century before World War I when industry began to penetrate into the decentralized, mountainous canton, farmers migrated to the valleys to work in factories. Farmers' families maintained the largely self-sufficient mountain farm. The economic pattern established at that time continued largely unchanged until the midtwentieth century in alpine regions of Switzerland.

However, in aluminum production, the Swiss work force was supplemented to a large extent by foreign workers. It cannot be proven conclusively that foreigners limited wage increases. Nonetheless, it can be concluded that the availability of foreign workers was of particular importance in establishing industry in a region lacking a concentrated, indigenous work force.

Building Materials

Foreigners performed role 1 in the manufacture of building materials in Switzerland, for they comprised a significant proportion of the factory work force. During the decade prior to World War I, 40 percent of the work force were foreign, originating, for the most part, from Italy.[96] With the employment of foreign laborers, the industry was able to shift production to large-scale operations and expand exports considerably (role 1).

Although the majority of products manufactured by the Swiss building materials industry supplied the home market, nevertheless exports of three building materials increased substantially during the period. Between 1888 and 1912, the value of exports of Portland cement rose from 53,000 Swiss francs to 1,551,000 Swiss francs. Exports of raw asphalt doubled, and exports of asbestos, which was not an export product in 1888, were valued at 1,791,000 Swiss francs in 1912.[97]

Foreign workers contributed significantly to the growth of exports. In brick works, cement works, and limestone quarries, foreigners were a large component of the work force.[98] During the first decade of the twentieth century, the industry transferred production to large-scale operations. In 1900, 65 percent of the total work force were employed in factories, whereas in 1910, 94 percent worked in factories.[99] Foreign workers accounted for 3,802 of the total 5,536 increase in the number of factory workers.

The industry was located primarily in the German-speaking region of Switzerland, in the cantons of Zurich, Bern, Aargau, Thurgau, St. Gall, and Schaffhausen. There were also cement works in the French-speaking canton of Vaud and asphalt works in Neuchâtel. Foreign workers were found throughout the industry except in the canton of Bern, which did not employ foreigners to any major extent.

The industry used the extensive reserves of raw materials in Switzerland. Granite was found in the cantons of Uri and Ticino and slate in the cantons of Glarus and Bern. Chalk, plaster, and marl were mined in the Jura mountains in western Switzerland, and asphalt was produced in the Val de Travers in Neuchâtel.[100]

Watchmaking

The Swiss watchmaking industry was the only manufacturing branch that did not employ foreigners to any significant extent during the prewar period. Whatever foreigners were employed came primarily from neighboring regions of France and worked in new watch factories in Switzerland.

Watch manufacture in Switzerland underwent a transformation in production techniques during the quarter-century preceding World War I. The transition from a workshop and cottage industry to a factory-based industry took place rapidly in response to competition from the United States.[101] New factories for manufacturing watches were established, especially in the Bern Jura. In 1888, only 20 percent of those employed in watchmaking worked in a factory. By 1911, the proportion of factory workers had increased to 62 percent.[102] During the same period, the value of watch exports doubled.[103]

Foreign workers, though few in number, worked for the most part in watch factories.[104] The cantons of Bern and Neuchâtel employed the largest number of foreigners in 1910. Professor Landes has pointed out that foreign labor might not have been so important in watch factories as in other Swiss factories because "the industry needed relatively little help from outside."[105] Swiss watch manufacturers engaged Swiss female labor and also moved to new regions of Switzerland where German-speaking, Catholic French-speaking, and Ticinese laborers were recruited.[106]

In Geneva, on the other hand, the foreign impact on the watch industry had been felt early and was still apparent at the beginning of the twentieth century. Foreign workers first appeared in the Geneva clock trade in the latter half of the sixteenth century, when Protestant refugees from Paris, Lyon, Lorraine, and Flanders brought their skills and manufacturing techniques to the city. Before the 1550s, only one clockmaker worked in Geneva. By 1600, after the first wave of immigration, there were twenty-five to thirty masters and an unknown number of workmen and apprentices.[107] In 1700, London and Geneva were the "two greatest centres of clock and watchmaking in Europe."[108]

By the beginning of the twentieth century, Geneva's position as a watchmaking center had diminished.[109] Factories in the cantons of Bern and Neuchâtel employed considerably more watchmakers. However, the proportion of foreigners employed in Geneva exceeded the proportions employed in the rest of Switzerland. Twenty-four percent of those working in watchmaking in Geneva in 1910 were foreign born.[110]

Conclusion

Foreigners performed what have been identified as roles 1 and 2 in Swiss manufacturing industries between 1888 and 1914. Foreigners enabled Swiss industry to introduce mass production processes (role 1), and foreigners formed one link in the interdependent industrial development of central European economic regions (role 2).

In Chapter 4, the principal roles that foreigners performed in specific manufacturing branches have been described. In most branches, several roles have been identified. However, in the metalworking and building materials branches, their impact appeared to be limited to role 1. Foreigners, employed as factory workers, were a supplementary work force that helped industries convert to large-scale, mass production operations. Since both of these branches supplied the domestic market, connections with other countries during the prewar period were not evident.

In the Swiss clothing industry, on the other hand, there was little indication of modernization before 1914. Foreigners working in this traditional, non-automated trade performed only role 2. They served as a link between Swiss garment production and developments in the rest of Europe. In the watchmaking industry, foreigners were of relatively minor significance and did not affect the growth of the industry during the prewar period. Neither role, therefore, was applicable to this branch. In other branches of manufacturing—shoes, food processing, chemicals, printing, and wood processing—foreigners performed a wide range of functions. Some of the activities were identified as fitting into role 1 and some into role 2.

5
FOREIGNERS IN THE SWISS TEXTILE INDUSTRY

During the quarter-century preceding World War I, foreigners working in textile production in Switzerland performed what has been described in this study as role 1: Foreign workers provided the labor force necessary for the introduction of mass production methods of manufacture.

Switzerland has been producing textiles for the world market for many centuries.[1] However, during the nineteenth century, traditional production methods were gradually superseded by machinery-operated factories. In some declining branches of textile manufacture, employment of foreign workers allowed the industry to continue producing textile products that were being replaced by international competitors. In the embroidery branch, foreigners were instrumental in establishing machine-produced embroidery exports. The impact of foreign workers on the growth of embroideries before World War I is analyzed in a special section later.

A case study of this traditional Swiss industry provides an opportunity to analyze the role of female foreign workers. Females, especially from northern Italy, were the main source of labor in Swiss textile factories.

Foreigners participated in the production of Swiss textiles as early as the sixteenth century, when the first wave of Protestant refugees from Catholic Europe migrated to Switzerland.[2] In Geneva, Calvin encouraged refugees to participate in the economy of the city.[3] Although there was some opposition to Calvin's hospitable policy, there were no autonomous craftsmen's organizations after 1541 that could officially stop foreigners from enjoying equal economic opportunity. Therefore, woolen handweavers from northern France and Flanders enlivened the Geneva wool trade, and Italian refugees tried to develop silk production in Geneva.

In Zurich, the reception accorded to foreigners in the 1500s was not nearly so friendly as in Geneva. Zurich's guilds, which wielded the

economic power in the city, feared potential competition from foreigners. Wide-scale unemployment during the midsixteenth century
further inflamed the population's antiforeign sentiments. Nonetheless,
by the latter part of the century, Protestant refugees mainly from Italy
were granted permission to manufacture silk in Zurich. Silk mills could
be operated only within the city, but they processed and exported goods
produced in farmhouses in the countryside. By 1600, silk and cotton
industries in Zurich were dominated by immigrants from Locarno.[4]
They imported raw materials from Venice and Bergamo in Italy and
established a cottage system of spinning and weaving in the Zurich
countryside. Bodmer described the "capitalistic, highly developed form
of production" as a northern Italian type, which, at the same time, was
prevalent in Milan, Venice, and Genoa.[5]

Basel, during the sixteenth century, received refugees who had failed
in Geneva or been expelled from Zurich.[6] Silk workers came in the 1560s
and 1570s, and lace makers (Posamentiere) from northern France and
Flanders came after 1571. However, in the early 1600s, the number of
restrictions imposed on the economic activities of refugees increased.
These drove a large number of foreign Protestant families out of the city
and into the canton of Basel Country, where they became outworkers in
a cottage system of production.

The next wave of immigration that affected the Swiss textile industry
occurred after the Edict of Nantes[7] was revoked in 1685. A large number
of Huguenots sought refuge in Switzerland in the late seventeenth and
early eighteenth centuries. According to Warren Scoville, there were
twenty-five thousand refugees living in Switzerland in the late 1600s.
They settled mainly in Geneva, Bern, Zurich, and the present canton of
Vaud in the vicinity of the city of Lausanne.[8] Even though there was
open antagonism and economic discrimination against their participation in the Swiss economy, nonetheless, their contribution to the Swiss
textile industry was substantial. The impact of Huguenots was especially
notable in printing cotton cloth, and silk and wool manufacture. The
Huguenots established factories, provided a work force of craftsmen,
and maintained links with other European textile centers and markets.
In Geneva, refugees faced considerable difficulties. According to
Scoville, "Louis XIV so cowed Geneva with dire threats of economic and
even military sanctions that before 1688 the city refused to accept any
Huguenots as inhabitants."[9] Afterward, their economic activities were
curtailed: They could sell goods at the fair only two days a week and
could not operate their own booths. Nonetheless, refugees took part in a
wide range of textile crafts, such as spinning silk thread, weaving silk
stockings, ribbons, fabrics, and taffetas. After 1700, wealthy Huguenots

set up a large-scale factory for printing cotton cloth; by 1785, the factory was employing two thousand workers.

Silk production expanded in all cities that foreigners inhabited. For example, in Lausanne, silk workers from Nîmes, France, established a silk manufactory. In Zurich, although forbidden to establish laundries or dyehouses, Huguenots started silk stocking factories in 1686 and 1689. Foreign entrepreneurs benefited from Switzerland's trade policies. In contrast to France, where excise duties on imported raw materials increased operating costs, there were no duties on raw silk or wool imports in Switzerland. The manufacture of wool stockings was also advanced by the Huguenots, who worked not only as skilled craftsmen but also constructed stocking-knitting looms. In addition, foreign craftsmen wove serges and coarser woolens.

Foreigners who migrated to Switzerland in the sixteenth and seventeenth centuries affected the textile industry in the same ways that later migrants in the nineteenth and twentieth centuries did. They acted as transmitters of new technology through their role as entrepreneurs; they provided a work force of hand-workers; and they helped integrate Swiss industry with commercial developments in the rest of Europe.

Although foreigners continued to play a part in the further development of the Swiss textile industry in the eighteenth century, there is no indication that new migrants exerted the types of influence previously described. Only in the nineteenth century when the mechanization of spinning and weaving transformed the production processes is there evidence again of an important role played by foreigners.

During the eighteenth century, the cottage system of textile production, thoroughly analyzed by Rudolf Braun,[10] consolidated itself as the primary method of producing cotton, silk, linen, and wool in Switzerland. Textile businesses headquartered in merchant houses in the city or town used the labor of outworkers spinning and weaving thread and cloth in their own farmhouses in the surrounding countryside. The factor (Fergger), who supplied raw materials and returned the finished material to the entrepreneur, became a central figure in the Swiss landscape. In the canton of Zurich in the second half of the eighteenth century, which, according to Braun, was one of the most intensively industrialized regions of Europe, approximately one-third of the rural population was employed in this system of textile production.[11]

The Swiss textile industry in the nineteenth century included the manufacture of several types of textiles, but it was cotton and silk that accounted for the dominant international reputation of Swiss textiles.

The Swiss cotton industry flourished in the nineteenth century. Cotton thread, woven white and colored cloths, printed cotton cloth, and embroideries were cotton goods that Switzerland produced competitively with the rest of the world. A later section of this chapter deals particularly with the history of the embroidery branch, since it was during the early twentieth century that embroideries attained the peak of productive capacity. Other branches of the cotton industry, however, were already in decline between 1888 and 1914.

Cotton spinning in Switzerland was mechanized for the most part by 1820.[12] Large spinning mills were located mainly in German-speaking eastern Switzerland, especially in the cantons of Zurich, Aargau, Thurgau, Glarus, and St. Gall. By 1844, there were 131 cotton-spinning factories, which employed a total of approximately 10,000 workers. At the height of spinning capacity in 1872, there were 21,000 spinning operatives in Switzerland.[13]

The international economic crisis in the 1870s, however, affected the Swiss cotton-spinning branch severely. According to Gruner, it "was the hardest hit of all branches of the textile industry."[14] The loss of markets to cheaper competitors forced the industry to contract quickly. In 1882, the number of spinning workers fell to 14,336, and by the outbreak of World War I, only eighty-three factories were still spinning cotton thread in Switzerland.[15]

In comparison with spinning, the cotton-weaving branch of the Swiss textile industry was a longer lived competitor in the international marketplace. In the 1880s, cotton weaving in Switzerland still employed thirty thousand workers.[16] The different fortunes that befell these two closely related branches of the textile industry may be credited to two causes. Firstly, cotton weaving in contrast to spinning was not fully mechanized by the late nineteenth century. In fact, in 1882–83, more than half of the cotton weavers in Switzerland were still weaving on handlooms.[17] Mechanization of cotton weaving was as unpopular in Switzerland as it had been elsewhere in Europe. Just as the Luddites in England, Swiss weavers resisted the introduction of power looms. The uprising and burning of the Corrodi and Pfister factory in Uster, Zurich canton, in 1832 by the work force brought the mechanization of cotton weaving "temporarily to a standstill."[18] Because it was not wholly mechanized, Swiss weaving was not directly in competition with the weaving industries of other countries. Secondly, the products that Switzerland sold were either high quality, handwoven cloth or one of the several specialties, such as satin stitch colored cloth, which Swiss weavers developed.

The other important branch of the Swiss textile industry in the nineteenth century was silk. Even though it suffered from many ups and downs during the hundred years between the end of the Napoleonic Wars and World War I, in 1914, silk goods were still the third most valuable Swiss export.[19] Woven silk products were the important export, for other divisions of the Swiss silk industry, such as silk spinning and raw silk production in Ticino, were already in decline by the end of the nineteenth century. Synthetic silk or rayon production, on the other hand, was still in its infancy.

Historically, silk weaving was associated with two centers in Switzerland. The city of Zurich and the neighboring countryside of canton Zurich formed a major region of concentration. The other region, Basel, the city and countryside extending into the German Duchy and later state of Baden, was the center for weaving silk ribbons. This business was not only important to the Basel economy in the nineteenth century but also led to the creation of a modern Basel industry. The chemical industry developed largely as an outgrowth of dyeworks, which had been established to dye silk ribbons. In Basel, as also in canton Zurich, the Swiss silk industry during the quarter century before World War I employed both outworkers in a cottage system of production and factory workers in large-scale operations.[20]

The Swiss textile industry in the nineteenth century is closely identified with Swiss entrepreneurs, Swiss cottage workers, and Swiss machinery manufacturers. However, contrary to traditional assumptions, it can be shown that foreigners exerted a strong impact on the industry. Although foreigners comprised only 15 percent of the total work force in Swiss textile production, they nonetheless represented a substantial number of foreign workers.[21] In fact, in 1910 the only Swiss industry that employed more foreigners was the construction industry.[22]

The country of origin of foreigners working in the Swiss textile industry changed during the quarter-century preceding World War I. Throughout the nineteenth century, the cotton industry in eastern Switzerland and silk ribbon manufacturers in Basel had employed Germans and Austrians in the "putting-out" system: Domestic cotton weavers working for St. Gall entrepreneurs lived across the border in the Austro-Hungarian Empire (that is, Vorarlberg). In western Switzerland, Basel silk merchants had established a far-ranging putting-out system, extending across the Rhine River into Baden in Germany. By the mid-nineteenth century, many domestic workers had migrated to work in Basel's silk ribbon factories.[23]

In the twentieth century, Italian foreign workers in large numbers entered the Swiss textile industry. During the second decade of the century, Italians were the most numerous foreign workers employed in Swiss textile factories.[24] Although the total number of workers in the early twentieth century was relatively stable, nonetheless the proportion of factory workers of foreign origin increased significantly.[25] Italians accounted not only for growth in the number of foreigners employed, but also for the total growth in textile factory employment in the first decade of the twentieth century. During a period when the number of Swiss textile factory workers was decreasing, the number of Italians was increasing.

Factory statistics reveal that some branches of the industry relied more on foreign labor than other branches. Although the cotton and silk branches did not employ so high a percentage of foreigners as did the wool or linen branches, they nonetheless employed a larger number of foreign workers.[26]

The silk industry, especially silk ribbon production in Basel, had always employed a sizable number of Germans. Only in the twentieth century, though, is there evidence of large numbers of Italians working in Zurich's silk factories.[27] In cotton weaving, foreigners had traditionally played a smaller role than in silk weaving. In this branch, too, it was only at the beginning of the century that Italians were a substantial component of the cotton factory work force.[28] In addition to the major branches of cotton and silk, a less relatively important branch of the Swiss textile industry, namely, wool, also witnessed an appreciable increase in Italians in its work force.[29] In 1911, 32 percent of those employed in Swiss wool factories were foreign. The textile factories for spinning and weaving wool were among the largest textile factories in Switzerland.[30] They were located for the most part in the cantons of Zurich and Solothurn.

How can the employment of foreigners in an industry that had been almost totally Swiss be explained? Why did foreigners, especially from Italy, enter the Swiss textile industry in such substantial numbers at the beginning of the twentieth century? The three reasons presented here are by no means the only explanations. They, however, take account of both the condition of the industry and the labor market. In other words, they are a synthesis of push and pull factors that have been described in chapters 3 and 4 as reasons why foreigners migrated to work in Switzerland.

Firstly, the Swiss textile industry in general at the end of the nineteenth century had surpassed its peak. As an employer and an exporter, it continued to play a major role in the Swiss economy, but other newer industries, such as the engineering industry, were rapidly gaining in importance. As a traditional industry, it faced severe competition from textile industries in other countries, making it especially receptive to courses of action that might reduce production costs. The introduction of young Italian women into the labor force offered one such cost-saving solution.

Secondly, during the quarter-century before World War I, the Swiss textile industry introduced new textile machinery that made a new labor force particularly appropriate. The new machines required less skill from the work force. Therefore, it was not only the growth of foreigners in the industry, but especially the growth of foreigners in textile factories that was significant.

Thirdly, during the prewar period internal conditions in northern Italy encouraged a major portion of the population to emigrate.[31] Not only did Italian males leave to work overseas, but Italian females also migrated to work in textile factories in Switzerland.

The first explanation, that a depressed industry recruited Italian workers as an attractive cost-saving solution to problems of competition, raises another question concerning the timing of the migration. If this were an attractive solution, why did the industry not try it earlier, for instance during the crisis of the 1870s? Why did the industry wait until the twentieth century to employ foreign workers?

Prior to the 1900s, there is considerable evidence that Swiss textile firms established subsidiaries in other countries when faced with economic difficulties. In 1812, a cotton industrialist from Zurich set up a textile factory in Salerno, south of Naples. In 1834, the firm operated five hundred cotton looms and employed thirteen hundred workers.[32] Similarly, "many entrepreneurs transferred during the period of decline, a part of their factories to neighboring foreign countries especially to north Italy where there were good water power, cheaper wages and a certain market."[33] Swiss industrialist Caspar Honegger established both a spinning and weaving factory in Kottern in the Allgäu in Bavaria as early as 1846.[34]

According to Bosshardt, Nydegger, and Allenspach, the primary motive for emigration of Swiss textile firms was to avoid tariff barriers.[35] However, in the previously cited cases, Swiss textile entrepreneurs did not wait until the erection of constricting tariffs to set up foreign factories. In the United States as well, a considerable number of silk factories were started by Swiss businessmen in the 1870s. The tariff on silk goods was not instituted until 1883.[36] Paterson, New Jersey, developed as a center of Swiss silk subsidiaries. Albin Wietlisbach began manufacturing silk thread and ribbons in 1879 as part of the Neuburger Braid Company. Jakob Horand and Son from Basel started a silk ribbon factory in 1872, and Johann Grisch manufactured silk handkerchiefs beginning in 1879. The Zurich firm Schwarzenbach-Landis had a branch in the nearby town of West Hoboken. By 1889, there were ninety-three silk factories in Paterson alone.[37]

Swiss textile firms continued to establish subsidiaries in other countries until the outbreak of World War I when "half of the Swiss-owned production capacity of the silk-weaving industry and cotton mills lay beyond our frontiers."[38]

Avoiding high tariff barriers was one motivation, but also important to manufacturers was access to a supply of raw cotton and raw silk as well as a supply of labor. Nonetheless, at the beginning of the twentieth century, migration to Switzerland by foreign workers provided an alternative to the established practice of production outside the country.

In Switzerland, as in most countries, a traditional reserve of labor for the textile industry had been the rural population in the eastern cantons. The traditional labor force had been heavily dominated by female workers, in some branches more than in others.[39] By the end of the nineteenth century, however, Swiss females who had previously worked in this industry were no longer available in so large a number as before. There were two reasons. Firstly, young women were attracted to newer types of employment. The number of women, for example, in tourism, shopkeeping, health care, education, and transport rose substantially during the first decade of the twentieth century.[40] For bourgeois young women, "schools for social work were typical further education institutes in the years before and after World War I."[41] However, office work, especially in banks, remained a male occupation.[42]

Secondly, Swiss women tended to avoid unskilled employment in factories. Apart from the embroidery branch, the number of Swiss women employed in textile factories during the first decade of the twentieth century decreased.[43] At the same time, the number of foreign women, especially from northern Italy, increased.

Another reason why foreigners became more numerous in Swiss textile factories during this period was that new textile machinery was being introduced. In the silk industry, for instance, it was only at the turn of the century that the replacement of hand weaving by mechanical weaving was completed.[44] Furthermore, both cotton spinning and weaving were becoming fully automatic. The Northrop automatic changing loom was produced by Rüti Machinery Works after the company's acquisition of a license in 1898.[45] Ring spinning, which became widespread during the latter part of the nineteenth century, was further improved with Swiss innovations. Rieter started manufacturing spinning machines with individual electric drives in 1899, for example.[46]

In order to operate these machines, less skill was required from the textile worker than previously. Bosshardt, Nydegger, and Allenspach described the equipment as "foolproof" and considered its adoption by the Swiss textile industry as a negative development. Observing the industry from the vantage point of the 1950s, they concluded that "the skilled labor force which had been a productive advantage for Switzerland in many cases has disappeared."[47]

A trend toward using the most modern capital equipment as well as employing foreign laborers has continued until the present day. Stoffel

AG manufactures cotton jean material for nearly one-fifth of the Western European market. Approximately four-fifths of the company's work force is foreign.[48]

A third reason why the Swiss textile industry was able to employ a sizable foreign labor force at the beginning of the twentieth century was the availability of Italian female workers. Even though the northern Italian economy was expanding during this period, there was still a large number of unemployed Italians. As argued in Chapter 3, the Italian government encouraged workers to migrate to Switzerland.

Of the total 84,706 Italian women reported to have been living in Switzerland in 1910, a large number had either accompanied Italian men or were children. Therefore, they cannot be included in the count of foreign workers. However, a large proportion of young foreign women aged fifteen to nineteen came without families, recruited directly by textile factories.[49] Swiss firms constructed special housing to accommodate these young single foreign women, who were mainly Italians entering the country on completing their fourteenth year.[50] In a report in 1910–11, factory inspector Rauschenbach described the purpose of the housing establishments: "to secure a steady number of young female workers; cheaper than others. . . . The educational purpose, which in some of the prospectus are placed in the forefront, are and remain according to our conviction matters of secondary importance."[51]

Swiss Embroideries and Foreign Workers

One branch of the textile industry that experienced notable growth during the quarter-century before World War I was embroidery. Not only did production, reflected in export statistics and the number employed, increase sharply, but methods of production were also revolutionized. Especially during the years from 1895 to 1920, when semiautomatic and fully automatic embroidery machines were introduced, mass-produced Swiss embroideries became a major export.[52] The impact of foreigners on the growth of this branch of Swiss textiles was extensive and can be observed in some detail.[53]

Embroidery in Switzerland has always been associated with St. Gall, the textile center in the eastern part of the country. This city grew in the Middle Ages into a trade and financial center with international links based on the linen trade. Trading houses, which had been established to market domestically manufactured linen and later cotton goods, diversified into embroideries during the eighteenth century. By the latter half of the 1700s, the embroidery business was a major employer in the town of St. Gall and in the surrounding countryside, which included the agricultural region of Appenzell (two half-cantons). By 1790, more than one-third of those employed in textile production were in the embroidery branch.[54] This first period of growth of Swiss embroideries was short lived, however: The Napoleonic occupation at the turn of the century eliminated cotton imports and cut off export markets.

The rebirth of Swiss embroidery in the nineteenth century differed in several ways from its earlier beginnings. In order to meet competition from French, Saxon, and Scottish embroideries, the Swiss industry reacted in its characteristic manner. It turned to adventurous marketing, machine production, and foreign workers. Experienced traders from St. Gall, long acquainted with international textile trade routes, looked abroad for new markets. Even though traditional European markets remained important, the United States became a new customer, and Swiss embroideries were also sold as decorations on Turkish turbans.[55] The Swiss embroidery industry not only expanded its markets, but also introduced machinery that increased the quantity of embroideries markedly. According to Thürer, a hand embroiderer could produce ten thousand stitches a day, whereas two people working on an embroidery machine could produce forty thousand stitches a day.[56] The early machines were hand operated and could easily be used in the outworkers' homes. Although there was some movement toward factory production using the new equipment, a majority of the embroidery was still produced under the putting-out system. "Thousands of farmhouses in northeast Switzerland were rebuilt in order to accommodate these embroidery machines."[57]

The St. Gall merchant, with the assistance of the new machine, extended the putting-out system of production. Not only did agents (that is, factors) contract work to outworkers in the cantons of St. Gall and Appenzell, but also to Austrians in Vorarlberg and Liechtenstein. In southern Germany, in the textile town of Ravensburg, Swiss firms were also to be found.

During the nineteenth century, Swiss embroideries were established as an important branch of the textile industry. It was not, however, until the end of the century that this branch was of major significance to the Swiss economy. By the beginning of World War I, embroideries had become the most valuable Swiss export.[58]

The sudden and enormous expansion of embroideries was the result of the introduction of the Schiffchenstickmaschine and the effect that this machine had on production methods. The adoption of this machine was responsible for transferring production to the factory, mass producing embroidery products, and the widespread employment of foreign workers.

The Schiffchenstickmaschine was invented by Isaak Gröbli from Gossau (St. Gall canton) in 1863. As with most inventions, the time that

Schiffchenstickmaschine of 1886. *(Photograph courtesy of Adolph Saurer Ltd. Arbon, Switzerland.)*

Schiffchenstickmaschine of 1905. *(Photograph courtesy of Adolph Saurer Ltd. Arbon, Switzerland.)*

elapsed between the original discovery and wide-scale adoption by the industry was very long. Gröbli won prizes at the Paris World Fair in 1867 and at the Vienna World Fair in 1873. It was not, however, until the mid-1890s that the invention was finally accepted by Swiss industry.[59]

This embroidery machine worked on the same principle as Howe's sewing machine, using a shuttle that could hold several embroidery needles at the same time. It differed from previously used hand embroidery machines in that it avoided the time-consuming operation of drawing an embroidery needle and thread back and forth through the cloth for each stitch. With the Schiffchenstickmaschine, embroidery was performed on one side of the cloth only, and thread was continually fed through a ball attached to the machine.[60]

Gröbli himself had been a factor (Fergger) in Oberuzwil in St. Gall canton in the embroidery industry. He had, therefore, been well aware of the shortcomings of hand embroidery machinery. With his machine, one person could embroider twenty-four times the quantity as with the old machine.[61]

The textile machinery company, J. J. Rieter & Cie. in Winterthur, showed an early interest in Gröbli's invention and invited him to work full time for them. Between 1863 and 1878, Gröbli was employed by Rieter, during which time he successfully improved the Schiffchenstickmaschine. In 1870, Rieter, together with J. Wehrli and Gröbli, established a mechanical embroidery factory in Wülflingen near Winterthur. For approximately ten years, this factory produced and exported unusual machine-manufactured embroideries, such as embroidered leather for the Bally shoe factory.[62]

However, other engineering companies were to benefit more from the invention of the Schiffchenstickmaschine and its widespread adoption by the Swiss embroidery industry. Such Swiss engineering companies as Martini in Frauenfeld and Saurer in Arbon began to market the machines in the 1880s. German firms, such as Voigt in Chemnitz and a Plauen engineering company, also produced competitive designs. In the 1890s, the Schnelläufer, produced by the Plauen firm was widely marketed in Switzerland.

The Schiffchenstickmaschine was not the final innovation, for Gröbli's son, Johan Arnold Gröbli invented an automatic embroidery machine in 1898.

The Swiss engineering firm Saurer in Arbon (canton Thurgau) started selling fully automatic embroidery machines in 1911. The Automat, which embroiderers feared would replace people, could produce one-third more embroidery than the Schiffchenstickmaschine.[63] In 1920, the Swiss embroidery industry was employing fifteen hundred Automat machines and only half as many factory workers as in 1911.[64]

Automat, embroidery machine of 1912. *(Photograph courtesy of Adolph Saurer Ltd. Arbon, Switzerland.)*

In the novel *Die Sticker* (The Embroiderer) by Elisabeth Gerter about her childhood in the embroidery district of Gossau in St. Gall canton, she described reaction to the Automat.

> This new discovery . . . will take us backwards after a few stable years. We are now so advanced, that the costly human ingredient in our production process can be considerably reduced. The Automat eliminates the embroiderer. Only a few cheap assistants are needed. It results in a gigantic saving . . . and an enormous increase in profit.[65]

Automatic embroidery equipment (both the Schiffchenstickmaschine and the Automat) required a motor in order to function. Individual cottages or farmhouses with no power source were therefore ill suited to the new machines. In fact, adoption of these machines by the Swiss embroidery industry was closely correlated with the growth of factory production.

Factories in the embroidery industry were never large sized. According to Thürer, "The large undertaking was always the exception."[66] Even in 1919, at the peak of automized embroidery manufacture, only two factories in Switzerland owned more than one hundred Schiffchenstickmaschine. The vast majority of factories operated with fewer than five machines. Compared with other types of Swiss textile factories, namely, silk, wool, and cotton, embroidery factories were small sized.[67]

With adoption of new machinery, the type of work required from the labor force also changed. "In the course of the transition from hand embroidery to hand embroidery machines to Pantographs [that is,

Schiffchenstickmaschine] to automatic embroidery machines, the qualifications of the workforce have been continuously reduced."[68] The demand for less-skilled embroiderers led directly to an increase in the number of female factory workers employed in the industry.[69] Factory inspector Wegmann went so far as to report that one factory manager said that half- and fully automatic embroidery machines were "too easy and too monotonous for men to operate."[70]

Not only was there an increase in the number of female workers, but in particular in the number of young women aged fourteen to eighteen employed in embroidery factories.[71]

> In large number we find children in the Schiffchenstick factories and here in the factories with automatic machinery in relatively larger number, because the embroiderers who are adult workers have fallen off. There are some businesses in which the work force consists of half children and youth under the age of eighteen.[72]

Employment of children in the embroidery industry was not an entirely new development. As early as 1882, a federal factory inspector reported that before and after school, children helped their parents with the threading (fädeln).[73] In Gerter's novel, children were often described as inattentive at school because they had stayed up most of the night helping their family embroider. It had long been realized that cottage embroidery was an employment in which child labor was severely abused.[74] Only in 1923 did the Swiss federal government successfully introduce legislation dealing with the problem.

Employment of children in factories was another matter, however. According to the factory act of 1877, children under the age of fourteen were not permitted to work in factories. Furthermore, youths (aged fourteen to eighteen) were specifically forbidden to work on Sundays or at night. Nonetheless, factory inspector reports written during the decade before World War I described many instances when these laws were not respected.

For example, in a small Schiffli embroidery factory in 1912 to 1913, three boys aged fourteen, fifteen, and sixteen were found working on the night shift. The factory owner reported to the factory inspector that he had solicited a doctor's advice before employing the youths. He quoted the doctor as saying,

> I think that this kind of employment over a long period of time must lead to vocational damage and health dangers and disadvantages. Since this job however should last only one quarter of a year the health problems either will not have developed or else those starting will be able to be repaired.[75]

Another example was reported of an embroiderer with three machines under the regulation of the factory act and twelve children. Only one boy in the family embroidered, since the others were too young to enter the "factory." Yet in all the surrounding houses, children were working in the embroidery business. The man whose three machines were under the jurisdiction of the factory law became "a sworn enemy of all laws."[76]

Not only did the Schiffchenstickmaschine make possible wide-scale employment of females and youths in the embroidery industry, but it also enabled the industry to employ a relatively large number of foreign workers. In 1911, 25 percent of the factory labor force in this branch of the textile industry were non-Swiss.[77]

Even though the number of foreigners was substantial, perhaps more disruptive to such a traditionally based industry was the fact that the foreigners came mainly from Italy. Previously, the putting-out system of embroidery production had employed foreigners in their own homes. Foreigners had been primarily Austrians in Vorarlberg and southern Germans. In the early 1900s, on the other hand, thousands of Italian women came to eastern Switzerland specifically to work in embroidery factories. "It involved mostly girls aged fourteen to twenty years, who as a rule were imported directly by the enterprise and were prized as a cheap work force.[78]

The speed with which the migration occurred as well as the cultural differences that the migrants introduced brought changes to established working and living patterns in the embroidery districts. Importation of large numbers of young women, for example, required constructing suitable housing facilities.

Many factories erected workers' hostels to accommodate foreign workers.[79] Such housing was not entirely unfamiliar in eastern Switzerland, for the first one had been constructed as early as 1858 in Rüti, canton Zurich. However, after 1900 this type of housing expanded considerably. The housing was usually built near the factory; it was clean and well fitted with amenities; that is, central heating, running water, modern toilets, and bathrooms. Although the rooms were small, the factory inspector in 1910–11 reported that not more than two-thirds of the hostels were fully occupied. "Only seldom did two girls sleep in one bed," he reported.[80]

Problems for the inhabitants were the costs of housing and the severity of the rules. Although an average wage for factory embroidery was 1.50 Swiss francs a day, the young women had to pay 80 to 100 rappen daily for room and board.[81] Normally, there was a house manageress, and in many cases, she was a Catholic nun. Rules were strict, so that as factory inspector, Rauschenbach explained, "Outside of working hours there existed certain controls."[82] Inhabitants usually helped with housework. Early bedtime at nine in the evening was imposed, and correspondence was carefully inspected.

With regard to employing children, the large population of foreign workers created additional misunderstandings. Examples cited by the factory inspector in district three invariably involved Italian children.

Rauschenbach reported that many factory managers misinterpreted child factory legislation when Italian children were concerned. Several were purported to have said to him that they thought the legislation referred only to children of Swiss nationality. They thought that foreign children, for example, of Italian nationality, were allowed to work in factories under the age of fourteen.[83]

Another problem that the factory inspector described was school attendance. It was mostly the children of foreigners, he reported, who ignored these laws. Girls under the age of fourteen were often found in embroidery factories and not at school.

Not only did young Italian women migrate to an unfamiliar country where a foreign language was spoken, but the religion in eastern Switzerland also differed from the religion in Italy. Embroidery factories were located mainly in the cantons of St. Gall, Thurgau, and Appenzell Ausser-Rhoden. Both Thurgau and Appenzell were largely Protestant cantons, whereas the population of St. Gall included a sizable Protestant minority.[84] Foreign workers, in contrast, were Catholics.

During the period from 1888 to 1910, the religious composition of several Protestant cantons in Switzerland changed, as revealed in the censuses.[85] The canton of Thurgau was a good example: Between the 1880s and 1910, the population of this canton became seven percent more Catholic and 12 percent more foreign.[86] Since foreigners were primarily Catholic,[87] the catholicization of the canton reflected among other factors the large population of foreign workers employed during the period. The foreigners did not all originate from Italy, but in the factories of Thurgau, Italians were the predominant foreign nationality.[88] Not only did Italian women work in embroidery factories, but Italian men also manned the growing number of engineering factories.

In Appenzell Ausser-Rhoden, the other Protestant canton important in factory embroidery manufacture, foreigners were not engaged to any large extent.[89] It can be assumed that this mountainous, small half-canton could not accommodate foreign women, speaking another language and practicing another religion.

Conclusion

Foreign workers employed in the Swiss textile industry during the quarter-century preceding World War I performed role 1: They enabled the industry to introduce mass production methods of manufacture. In declining branches of textile production, cotton spinning and weaving, and silk weaving, foreigners were a replacement work force. Unable to attract a sufficient supply of Swiss female labor and prohibited from employing child labor, the industry recruited an outside reserve of factory workers—young Italian women.

In the case of the embroidery branch, however, foreign workers were engaged in a growing, dynamic industry. They were introduced along with new machinery that transformed Swiss embroideries from a skilled handicraft into a mass production industry.

6

FOREIGNERS IN THE SWISS ENGINEERING INDUSTRY

This case study of the engineering industry provides a close examination of the ways in which foreigners, who were for the most part men from Germany, contributed to the growth of a relatively new Swiss industry.[1] The engineering industry in Switzerland in the nineteenth century encompassed a broad range of machinery production, including the manufacture of textile machinery, hydraulic machinery, steam engines and turbines, locomotives, electrical and power generation equipment, milling, papermaking and woodworking machinery, agricultural equipment, and weapons.

From the beginning of the industry in the early nineteenth century until the outbreak of World War I, the impact of foreign technology, capital, trade, and labor will be shown to have been considerable. Foreign labor in particular, which amounted to 18.5 percent of the total work force in 1910,[2] will be shown to have affected the growth of output and the course of industrial relations.

However, the case study is more than a discussion of foreign labor; it is also a study of the wide-ranging German connection with this Swiss industry. By examining archives of several major Swiss firms, it was found that foreign workers from Germany were only one linkage in the association that developed between the two countries' engineering industries. For some companies, the role of German capital, technology, or management was more substantial than the role of German labor, but in all instances, close links between the two industries were evident. The early history of Brown, Boveri & Co. at the end of the chapter demonstrates the extent of interdependence among Swiss and German engineering firms.

The Swiss engineering industry had emerged as an important branch of Swiss industry by the early twentieth century. Measured in terms of the number of workers employed and the value of machinery exported, the industry had attained a leading role. At the outbreak of World War I, the Swiss engineering industry employed more workers in factories than any other Swiss industry, with the exception of textiles.[3] The value of Swiss machinery exports by 1912 had not yet approximated the value of textile or watch exports.[4] However, in 1912, machinery exports amounted to 9 percent of total manufactured goods exported by Switzerland.

This industry was located for the most part in the German-speaking region of Switzerland, especially in the cantons of Zurich, Aargau, Schaffhausen, St. Gall, and Bern. There was also machinery production in Geneva, especially of scientific instruments.[5]

Beginnings of the Engineering Industry

Engineering production in Switzerland experienced a slow, gradual growth, starting at the beginning of the 1800s. Origins were two-pronged, although many companies grew up simultaneously in both directions. One branch developed from requirements created by the mechanization of the Swiss textile industry. The need to repair foreign machines led to the indigenous manufacture of spinning and weaving machines and to more specialized textile machinery, such as knitting and embroidery machines.

The other path of development was via iron mining and foundries. Nearly all the early firms established their own foundries, so that they would have a supply of cast goods readily available.[6] During the mid-nineteenth century, the country's own reserves of iron, located in the Jura mountains (west of Delemont), in Fricktal (canton Aargau), and the largest reserves in Gonzen in eastern Switzerland near the present-day city of Sargans, supplied nearly half of the total demand for iron.[7]

By 1850, seventy-three engineering companies were in existence,[8] employing approximately three thousand workers.[9] With the opening of the Swiss Federal Institute of Technology in Zurich in 1855, Switzerland was able to provide for the first time the technical education required to train a professional class of engineers.[10] Accordingly, from that time on, the industry expanded rapidly. By the 1870s, there were thirteen firms in the German-speaking region of Switzerland alone, each of which employed more than two hundred workers.[11] Alongside the large engineering companies, there also developed a growing number of small engineering workshops, many of which were started by foreigners.[12] The actual number of Germans who worked in the Swiss engineering industry during this early period is difficult to estimate, but it was widely mentioned that skilled German mechanics, carpenters, and foundrymen from southern Germany worked in Switzerland as journeymen.[13]

Several Swiss firms recorded employing foreigners in the mid-nine-teenth century, but references were minimal. Maschinenfabrik Rüti (can-ton Zurich), founded by Caspar Honegger in 1842 to make weaving machines, employed foreigners in the early years.[14] The iron foundry Ludwig von Roll recruited skilled German foundrymen in 1854.[15] Sulzer Brothers in 1836, two years after its founding, employed twelve Prussian journeymen out of a total work force of eighteen.[16] Escher Wyss, the first Swiss engineering company, employed 112 Germans out of a total work force of 1,309 in 1873.[17]

It was during the early period that foreigners, mainly German but also English, contributed technical expertise to the nascent Swiss industry. The Winterthur firm Sulzer Brothers, in particular, was able to use technological discoveries made by foreign engineers. This company brought the Englishman Charles Brown to Switzerland in the 1850s. Brown, who was born in 1827 and educated in England, came to Sulzer Brothers while still in his twenties to set up a steam engine division. He went on to help found another Swiss engineering company in Win-terthur, the Swiss Locomotive and Machine Company, in 1871 and started the electrical engineering department at Maschinenfabrik Oerlikon in the 1880s. One of his sons, also named Charles Brown, later established the Swiss electrical engineering company, Brown, Boveri & Co.

This company also employed the young German engineer Rudolf Diesel in 1879. By the early twentieth century, Sulzer Brothers was a major producer of diesel motors, even though Rudolf Diesel had stayed with the firm for only a short time.[18] Sulzer also began manufacturing refrigeration machines in 1877, based on collaboration with Professor Carl von Linde from Munich Technical University. Professor von Linde, who was born in Berndorf, Bavaria, in 1842, attended the Swiss Federal Institute of Technology from 1861 to 1864. His patent for the ammonia refrigerator was granted in 1876.

Other Swiss engineering companies also used the technical expertise of foreigners during the early period. Escher Wyss recruited two English engineers, Lloyd and M. M. Jackson, to set up steamship production in the 1840s. The early history of Maschinenfabrik Oerlikon was closely associated with both English and German engineers. In 1863, the same Englishman Jackson who had been employed by Escher Wyss helped cofound Maschinenfabrik Oerlikon's predecessor. The German engineer F. A. Siewerdt was technical administrator of the company in the 1870s and 1880s.

By the end of the nineteenth century, the Swiss engineering industry had transformed itself into a firmly established factory-based industry.[19] Small family businesses that faced competition from English, German,

French, and American firms were increasingly converted into joint stock companies in order to expand production. In 1883, employers formed a machine industrialists association *(Verein schweizerischer Maschinenindustrieller)*, and in 1888, the work force organized a trade union in the industry *(Metallarbeiterverband)*.

In the decade and a half before World War I, the electrotechnical branch of the engineering industry tended to dominate the production schedules of major Swiss companies. Electricity-generating machinery, steam turbines, power stations, and machinery for the electrification of railways were major exports. Nonetheless, traditional products, such as textile equipment, milling machinery, and water power generators and pumps continued to be exported as well. In the years immediately preceding World War I, gas and pressurized-air engines were significant export products.[20]

German Connection

The impact of foreigners, predominantly of German origin, on the Swiss engineering industry increased significantly during the quarter-century before World War I. Not only did individual Germans contribute entrepreneurial and technical skills, but German raw materials, machine parts, and capital were also imported to a much greater extent than previously. The German connection became so strong that in the early twentieth century, several Swiss engineering firms merged with German enterprises. German capital was instrumental in establishing the Swiss electrical engineering branch. In 1895, the Bank für Elektrische Unternehmungen (Elektrobank) was set up in Zurich. German financiers contributed 76 percent of the original share capital, and in 1898, the bank was 95 percent German financed.[21] Swiss firms, such as Maschinenfabrik Oerlikon and Brown, Boveri & Co., were partly financed by the bank.

The firm Maschinenfabrik Oerlikon provides an example of the extensive German connection with the Swiss engineering industry.[22] In the case of this company, links with Germany dated back to the firm's founding in 1876. The first technical administrator was a German engineer, Friedrich Adolf Siewerdt, who came to Switzerland in 1863 to work at Bell & Co. in Kriens near Lucerne. He was originally from Waldenburg in Saxony and had been educated at the Werkmeisterschule in Chemnitz. In 1867, he formed a machine tool factory in Rorschach (canton St. Gall) together with another young engineer, Gustav Daverio, who came from northern Italy. Siewerdt's contacts with the German armaments industry made it possible for the Swiss company to receive orders for military machinery during the Franco-Prussian War.[23] Connections between Maschinenfabrik Oerlikon and the German engineering industry expanded rapidly when, in the 1880s, the firm set up an electrical engineering division under the management of Charles Brown senior. In 1889, the firm became a licensee of the German electrical company Allgemeine Elektrizitätsgesellschaft (AEG). In 1899, when share capital was increased, the company was nearly absorbed by the German group.[24] Although this did not happen, Emil Rathenau, general director of AEG, was elected to the board of directors of Maschinenfabrik Oerlikon.

Another Swiss engineering company, Escher Wyss of Zurich, was financially controlled by German capital between 1889 and the outbreak of World War I.[25] At the end of the nineteenth century, it was the largest Swiss engineering firm. It was founded in 1805 to manufacture spinning machinery and converted into a joint stock company in 1889. The German capital connection was used in developing the firm's Zoelly steam turbine in the early twentieth century. Henry Zoelly, technical manager of the company, invented a steam turbine that was manufactured by a syndicate consisting at first of only German companies but was later joined by a large number of international engineering firms.[26]

Not only capital for the engineering industry, but also trade in both raw materials and finished machinery became closely linked with Germany. Switzerland grew increasingly dependent on iron imports from Germany as her own reserves became uneconomic to exploit. In 1911, 29 percent of all Swiss raw material imports originated from Germany.[27]

However, it was not only iron and other industrial raw materials that were imported: Switzerland increased its imports of German machines and machine parts substantially as well. In 1912, 76 percent of imported machinery came from Germany, whereas only 18 percent of Swiss exports of machinery and machine parts went to Germany.[28]

Role of Foreign Labor

It was only during the two decades before World War I that foreign workers had a measurable impact on the development of the engineering industry. In 1910, foreigners comprised 18.5 percent of the total work force, and in 1911, they represented 17 percent of factory-employed labor.[29]

During the early twentieth century, several firms, as well as the industry as a whole, reported chronic labor shortages. According to the annual reports of the Association of Swiss Trade and Industry (Vorort), shortages of workers were so extensive that a large number of firms in 1907 were unable to take full advantage of the favorable business climate.[30]

The employment of foreign workers helped alleviate problems of labor supply. In Winterthur (canton Zurich), where Rieter Machine Works in 1900 had problems recruiting qualified workers,[31] Lotmar found that in 1905 approximately 10 percent of the workers in the engineering industry were foreign.[32] Engineering companies in the canton of Schaffhausen, which borders Germany, were able to engage Germans relatively easily during shortfalls in labor supplies. In 1910, foreigners comprised 40 percent of the work force in the engineering industry in Schaffhausen.[33] In one engineering firm in Schaffhausen, Georg Fischer AG, more than half of the work force was foreign in 1911.[34]

However, the engineering industry in the canton of Zurich, in which nearly 3,000 foreign workers were employed, had the largest number of foreigners in 1910. Other cantons where more than five hundred foreigners were employed in engineering were Schaffhausen, Geneva, Thurgau, Aargau, and St. Gall.[35]

During the two decades that preceded World War I, both the quantity of machinery exports and the number of foreign workers increased substantially. Although it is impossible to prove that foreign workers alone were responsible for the growth in exports, nonetheless it is possible to show some connection between the two phenomena.

Between 1895 and 1901, the number of foreign workers employed in the Swiss engineering industry increased 49 percent. Between 1901 and 1911, the number of foreign workers rose 62 percent. In the case of machinery exports, measured in quantity, the proportional increases during the same decades were 52 percent and 59.5 percent.[36]

An expansion in production during the early twentieth century required an expansion of the work force. Swiss employers were able to engage foreigners as an addition to the work force, as documented in Swiss factory statistics. Foreigners represented 22 percent of the total increase in factory workers in the engineering industry during the first decade of the century.[37]

Furthermore, it may be suggested that foreign workers were an economic means of expanding the work force. By examining wage and price data, it can be seen that during the two decades preceding World War I, wages of workers in the Swiss engineering industry rose more slowly than prices of housing and food.

There are various estimates of wages paid to engineering workers in Switzerland in the early twentieth century. The Swiss Machine Industrialists Association reported average earnings in 1905 of 4.40 Swiss francs a day.[38] G. de Michelis published wage rates for metalworkers in 1909, which ranged between three and six Swiss francs for a ten-hour day.[39] Siegenthaler's data permit a comparison of wages over time.[40] He showed that in the decades before foreign workers were employed widely in the Swiss engineering industry (that is, before 1900), wages rose faster than in the early 1900s.

Furthermore, in an examination of wage rates in the Swiss engineering industry in Winterthur (canton Zurich) during the early twentieth century, evidence of wage rate stability was also observed. Lotmar found that median wages paid in the engineering companies of Winterthur in 1905 were 4.20 Swiss francs per day for an average workday of ten hours.[41] In 1910, a majority of workers at Sulzer Brothers, the largest engineering firm in Winterthur, were still earning less than five Swiss francs per day. Out of a total work force of 2,573, there were 1,737 workers earning less than five francs and 836 earning more.[42]

Even though the period was one of meager wage rises in the Swiss engineering industry, consumer price movements, in contrast, were considerable. According to statistics gathered by the Swiss Metalworkers' Union, average rents for a two- to three-room apartment during the years 1904 to 1909 rose 17 percent. In some cities where the engineering industry was a major employer, rent increases were even more substantial.[43] Food prices similarly rose sharply in the first decade of the twentieth century. According to the Swiss Typographical Union, the average increase during the period was again 17 percent.[44] Although the connection between the increase in the number of foreigners employed and the stagnation of wage rates may not have been one of direct cause and effect, the fact remains that the two occurrences took place during the same time period.

Foreigners and Industrial Relations

Foreign workers from both Germany and Italy were an important reserve of labor for the Swiss engineering industry during a period of rapid expansion. Foreign workers from Germany also exerted a strong impact on the development of worker and employer relations in the industry. Foreigners were prominently represented in the leadership and membership of workers' associations and in industrial actions during the early twentieth century.

Industrial relations in Switzerland were altered permanently during the interwar period. The Peace Agreement of 19 July, 1937 established a no-strike policy, which has remained in effect into the 1980s. This uniquely Swiss document was written by a representative of the trade union and the employers' association in the engineering industry.[45] The agreement was negotiated during a period when foreign workers were not numerous in Swiss engineering factories. In 1930, there were 7,857 foreigners and 89,429 Swiss employed in the industry, and in 1941, there were 4,853 foreigners and 129,190 Swiss employed. In contrast, during the early twentieth century when foreigners were prevalent, Swiss industrial relations were closely associated with policies in Germany.

In 1906, the Swiss employers' association in the engineering industry published a study, which it had commissioned, by a Swiss lawyer, Dr. Hermann Meyer, on the labor movement in the industry. Although the report reflected the bias of engineering employers, nonetheless it gives an indication of the extent of association that existed between the Swiss and German labor movements.

> The correspondence of the fundamental demands, as well as the synchronism of urging these demands in both Germany and Switzerland led me to conclude with assurance that the recent movement in the Swiss engineering industry is not independent from events that originated in Germany. Either the Swiss metalworkers union has adopted from its older German brother its fundamental demands or else has set them up in association with them. One recognizes in the large number of Germans acting as agitators in Switzerland that intensive mutual relationships exist between the general Swiss trade union movement and the German movement that is considered a model. And the Swiss Metalworkers' Union see perhaps more than other trade unions salvation in connection with foreign trade unions. According to article 2 of its statutes, it will achieve its goals, moreover, through "Attention to Internationalism through respect of the reciprocal principles of the freedom to live where one likes and union with the international secretariat of the metalworkers."[46]

Foreigners comprised a large portion of the membership in the major trade union in the engineering industry, the Metalworkers' Union *(Metallarbeiterverband),* which was formed in 1888.[47] (This union is part of the Swiss Trade Union Federation *(Schweizerische Gewerkschaftsbund SGB,* which itself was established in 1880). Even though the union never represented a majority of the work force in the engineering industry, nonetheless there was a significant growth in membership during the quarter-century before World War I. The number of members increased from one thousand in the early 1890s to nearly eighteen thousand in the peak membership year, 1908. This meant that in 1895, only 6 percent of those employed in the engineering industry were in the union. By 1901, the proportion had risen to 13.5 percent, and in 1911, nearly 30 percent of the workers in the engineering industry belonged to the union.

Germans were the only nationality of foreign worker to participate to any significant extent in this Swiss trade union. The German presence, however, was short lived, for by 1914, Swiss workers constituted the overwhelming majority of union members.[48]

Many of the leaders of the Swiss trade union movement were also German born. Meyer referred to these men as "Germans acting as agitators in Switzerland." Several labor leaders, such as Hermann Greulich, Emil Beck, and Robert Seidel, however, were more Swiss than German, for they had settled in Switzerland as young men.[49] Meyer's description did not accurately apply to them. Their contribution to the Swiss labor movement was solidly based on consideration of Swiss industrial conditions. Nevertheless, many of the policies they advocated were similar to those of the German labor movement. Other labor leaders, such as Emil Hauth and Willi Münzenberg, who worked in Switzerland only a few years, and the German Social Democrats, who published a newspaper in Zurich during the 1880s, were more closely connected to German politics. There is every indication that Swiss politicians and trade unionists who had been in contact with these Germans were directly influenced by their writings and ideas.

The impact of foreign ideas on the development of trade unionism in the Swiss engineering industry is evident in the strike that took place in Winterthur in the summer of 1910 at Rieter Machine Works. It spread to Sulzer Brothers and lasted nearly one and a half months.[50] Industrial action began on Saturday, 4 June, when ten unskilled assistants at the Rieter foundry handed in their notices to leave the firm. On the same day, as a result of the action by the ten assistants, the company issued dismissal notices to six skilled foundrymen. In a collective response, eighty-six foundry workers also handed in their notices to the management.[51]

Motives for the strike were the unresolved working conditions at the new Rieter foundry, in operation since July 1908. Previously, Rieter had purchased cast materials mainly from Sulzer's foundries. With the introduction of the Rieter foundry, however, countless problems had occurred. The company had difficulty recruiting a work force. There had been endless delays in construction, and inadequate provision was made for the health and welfare of the work force. Pay schedules and piece rates had remained unsettled. All the problems had created a general environment of noncooperation between employers and workers. At the beginning of 1910, a number of issues had been raised by the Metalworkers' Union Winterthur branch. The union was particularly concerned about unsafe working conditions and unresolved piece rates. The company, however, took no action.

On 18 June, 1910, strikers presented in writing their specific demands to Rieter management. They were

1. Increased hourly wages
2. Special pay increases for unskilled assistants
3. Abolition of piecework reductions and guarantee of 65 rappen per hour for piecework

4. Mutual agreement on rates for piecework
5. Piecework rates and time books to be written in ink
6. Installation of ventilators
7. Reconstruction of the combustion system in the drying oven
8. Reduced working time

Rieter management refused all demands with the exception of 4 and 5, which they said had already been granted before the strike began. Nonetheless, each of the points has a history. A further explanation will provide a basis for determining whether Rieter foundrymen were influenced by demands put forth by trade unionists in Germany during the same period.

The demands concerning pay applied to both the special conditions at Rieter Machine Works and general changes that were taking place in the engineering industry in Germany and Switzerland. It was common practice to pay reduced piecework rates because machine tools increased the productivity of skilled workers. It was also common practice to pay unskilled workers (odd jobbers in the foundry) by the hour, since the work did not consist of filling orders. However, at Rieter Machine Works, when piece rates were reduced, total earnings of foundrymen did not necessarily rise, since productivity was not so high as in other foundries in Winterthur.[52] Productivity was lower at Rieter for two reasons: Firstly, the firm had found it difficult to recruit a skilled work force, so workers employed may not have been the best foundrymen. Secondly, inadequate working conditions at the foundry may have reduced productivity.

Demands 6 and 7 directly concerned problems with working conditions. Ventilation in the foundry had been a subject of controversy since the opening of the foundry. Previously, the Arbeiterkommission (workers' commission) had demanded the installation of ventilators, but the company had refused claiming that "the ventilation was not bad."[53] However, at the end of 1909, four foundry workers had nearly died from carbon monoxide poisoning.[54] When the issue was raised again during the strike, the company again refused, explaining that the wall on which the ventilators were to be installed was intended to be removed. The company's reply to the strike demand for a combustion system in the drying oven was another example of delaying a solution to a working condition problem. Although the firm said that it had constructed better arrangements for firing the drying oven, nevertheless, the work force wanted the oven to be fired outside the building.[55] In February 1910, when the Metalworkers' Union had suggested introducing a second crane in the foundry, management had similarly found reasons for procrastination.[56]

The final strike demand concerning a reduction in working hours was commonly raised in strikes during the early twentieth century regardless of the country or industry in which the strike was taking place. In this case, with a normal workday of ten hours, the union demanded a reduction to nine hours. This was not achieved until the end of World War I. It could be concluded, therefore, that the demands put forth by the striking foundrymen in Winterthur in 1910 were both specific to conditions at Rieter Machine Works and yet consistent with more general confrontational tactics that were part of industrial relations in both Switzerland and Germany before the First World War.

The strike at Rieter Machine Works spread to Sulzer Brothers on 21 June when 140 foundrymen at Sulzer joined the strike.[57] They refused to supply cast goods from their foundry while the Rieter foundry was on strike. These strikes were not limited to the companies' foundries, for without cast materials, the mechanical workshops of both companies were forced to curtail production, causing a considerable number of layoffs. The strike lasted until 30 July. Both firms agreed to reinstate most of the striking workers, although in each company, this was the subject of intensive negotiation. In Sulzer Brothers, twenty strikers were not reemployed, and at Rieter, twenty-four were not reemployed.[58] The management of Rieter Machine Works stated in the 1910 annual report that the strike had ended "with a complete defeat of the Organisation [i.e., trade union]."[59] However, foundry output at Rieter was reduced in 1910–11, creating a considerable loss to the firm.[60]

The account of one particular strike is not sufficient proof that a strong connection existed between German and Swiss trade unions in the engineering industry. However, the similarity of demands, the international perspective of the Swiss Metalworkers' Union, and the large preponderance of Germans in the work force of the engineering industry provide specific indications of extensive contacts between trade unionists of the two countries.

In some towns and in some companies in the Swiss engineering industry, these connections may have been more or less direct. In Winterthur, the proportion of foreigners in the work force was only 10 percent, whereas in towns nearer to the German border, proportions were considerably higher. Nonetheless, it was reported that among foundrymen in the Winterthur engineering industry, there were a large number of German origin.[61] Since this strike started in the Rieter foundry, it could safely be assumed that the work force was familiar with German trade union strategies and perhaps influenced by them. Furthermore, it should be remembered that this strike was carried out under the leadership of the Swiss Metalworkers' Union. Germans participated actively in this union during the early twentieth century. At the end of 1909, 16 percent of the membership of this union was German.[62]

Case Study of Brown, Boveri & Co.

It is possible to observe the specific roles played by foreigners in the development of the Swiss engineering industry by examining the history of the early years of the electrical engineering firm, Brown, Boveri & Co. This company, which was founded in 1891 in the town of Baden in the canton of Aargau, has retained an important position in the Swiss engineering industry.[63]

The firm provides an especially suitable case study. Its early history demonstrates the kind of association that existed between engineering industries in the German-speaking cantons of Switzerland and the southern region of Germany during the quarter-century before World War I. The technological, financial, and labor cooperation between the two countries was intensive.

The two cofounders of the company, Walter Boveri and Charles Eugene Lancelot Brown, were both closely associated with the German engineering industry. Walter Boveri was born in Bavaria and educated at the Royal School of Engineering in Nuremberg. He met Charles Brown at Maschinenfabrik Oerlikon where Boveri went to work as an engineer in 1885. Although Boveri married into a prominent Zurich family[64] and became a Swiss citizen in 1893, his contacts with Germany were used extensively during the early years of the firm's history. His cousin from Bavaria, Fritz Funk, was the original business manager of the firm and a member of the board of directors in 1906. Boveri's German background provided access to the Germany military, for the firm sold steam turbines for ships to the German Navy in the 1900s. In 1912, when Boveri acceded to the presidency of the firm, on the retirement of Charles Brown, contacts with German mining and metal industries intensified.[65]

Charles Brown, although English in origin,[66] spent his childhood in Switzerland and received his technical education at the Technical College in Winterthur. His early engineering achievements at Maschinenfabrik Oerlikon, where he assumed management of the electrical engineering department in 1884 from his father, were well known in Germany. His successful transmission of direct electricity for a distance of 8 kilometers in 1886 was well publicized. In 1889, Brown built a single-phase power transmission plant in Kassel, Germany, and in 1891, while still working for Maschinenfabrik Oerlikon, he was responsible for long-distance power transmission from Lauffen to Frankfurt.

By the time Brown formed his own firm with Walter Boveri, the

Brown, Boveri & Co., Swiss engineering company in Baden, Switzerland. *(Photographs by the author.)*

former's engineering reputation brought immediate contacts with German engineers. Brown's talent was recognized, for instance, by the Frankfurt city engineer W. H. Lindley. Although Brown was a foreigner, he was able to win a contract for his new company to supply generators to the Frankfurt-am-Main power station in 1893.[67]

Not only did the founders of the firm have German backgrounds or connections, but investment capital also came in large measure from Germany. The company grew quickly in the 1890s, so that in 1900, the demand for capital necessitated conversion from a limited liability company into a joint stock firm. A seven-member board of directors *(Verwaltungsrat)*[68] was appointed with C. E. L. Brown as president and Walter Boveri as vice-president. Representatives from German financial institutions assumed prominence on the firm's board of directors during the prewar period. Two German citizens, Max Huth of the Allgemeine Deutschen Creditanstalt Leipzig and Dr. Paul Roediger of Frankfurt-am-Main, served as members of the original board of directors. Four years later in 1904, the board was enlarged to eleven members and included five Germans. Walter Rathenau joined the board at that time, a position he held until 1914. Two representatives from the Allgemeine Elektrizitätsgesellschaft (AEG) in Berlin, Felix Deutsch and J. Hamspohn, also joined the board of Brown Boveri in 1904. They each served five years until 1909 to 1910. Another board member, Julius Frey, came from the Bank für Elektrische Unternehmungen (Elektrobank) in Zurich. This bank was mainly German financed.[69] By 1911, German representation on the board of directors had declined: On the fifteen-member board only four members were German.

As the firm expanded the size of its board of directors and its supplies of investment capital, the labor force grew as well. Beginning in 1891 with sixty-two employees, Brown, Boveri & Co. employed 3,166 in 1914.[70] Although specific data about the nationality of workers are unknown, it has been possible, nevertheless, to reach some conclusions about the likelihood of foreigners in the work force based on other types of evidence.[71]

Industrial employment opportunities were very limited in Baden in the nineteenth century. Apart from a spinning factory, which employed mainly women and children, there were two small beer breweries and several small mechanical workshops. The firm of Oederlin, which employed three hundred workers by 1900, grew to specialize in armaments manufacture. The other metalworking factory, Merker, was started by an immigrant German in 1873 to make household goods.[72]

Since there are no statistics available on the number of foreign workers employed by Brown Boveri before World War I, official Swiss census data offer the only clue to understanding where the work force may have

originated. Because there were no major competitors in Baden for industrial labor, it can be assumed that foreigners who did migrate to Baden
were in all likelihood employed by Brown, Boveri & Co. Comparing
census data for Baden in the years 1888, 1900, and 1910, it can be seen
that the numbers of foreigners increased markedly. In 1888, three years
before the founding of the firm, only 1 percent of the town's population
was foreign born.[73] By 1900, when the firm's work force had expanded to
1,320, the population of Baden had become 18 percent foreign.[74] In the
1910 census, the foreign population of Baden had increased to 21.5
percent, still predominantly of German origin.[75]

This is not the only evidence to suggest that foreigners from Germany
comprised a part of the work force at Brown, Boveri & Co. The company
decided to set up a subsidiary manufacturing branch in Mannheim in
1898 only seven years after its founding. Here it was possible to employ
Germans directly in machinery production without recruiting them to
work in the Swiss factory. In 1905, the work force at Brown Boveri
Mannheim had surpassed one thousand,[76] and in 1910, the subsidiary
had acquired another electric company in Saarbrucken. The Mannheim
subsidiary was the first factory established by Brown Boveri outside
Switzerland, but others in France, Italy, Norway, England, and Austria
were started before the outbreak of World War I.

Not only were capital and labor closely linked to Germany, but the
company's market was also largely dependent on Germany. During the
first decade of the firm's history, in the 1890s, orders for generators from
German power stations were essential. In 1901, the company reported
that sales in Switzerland amounted to not more than one-fifth of total
production. The report listed fifteen major orders and deliveries during
that year, five of which were German. In 1902, three out of the total nine
deliveries of turbogenerators went to Germany. Manufacture of steam
turbines, a new product in the early twentieth century, was from the
outset export orientated. In 1903, the company reported an order to
supply steam turbines to the German Navy. The contract with the
German Navy continued until 1908 when Brown Boveri's steam turbines
were used on the cruiser Stettin and the high seas torpedo boat G137.[77]
Between 1909 and 1924, the company had controlling participation in a
German shipbuilding firm Howaldtswerke AG in Kiel.[78]

Conclusion

It can be concluded from the foregoing that foreigners, especially of
German origin, had considerable impact on the development of the
Swiss engineering industry. Not only foreign labor, but also foreign

technology, foreign capital, foreign raw materials, and foreign markets were vitally important to the growth of the new industry.

During the prewar period, connections between the engineering industries of Switzerland and Germany were so extensive that the histories of several Swiss companies became inseparable from the history of the German engineering industry.

7
FOREIGNERS IN NONMANUFACTURING INDUSTRIES

The impact of foreign labor on the development of Swiss manufacturing industries was extensive, as analyzed in preceding chapters. However, some nonmanufacturing industries in Switzerland also employed a considerable number of foreign workers. The construction industry was the single largest employer of foreign workers, and domestic service was the second largest employer of foreigners in 1910. Other service industries, such as tourism, commerce, entertainment, health care, and education, also employed sizable numbers.

This chapter describes the roles that foreigners played in construction work, services, and the primary sector of the Swiss economy. Comparatively few foreigners worked in Swiss agriculture during the pre-World War I period, even though a majority of migrants originated from agricultural backgrounds. In all the industries described in this chapter, foreigners performed traditional functions: They either replaced Swiss laborers or continued to be employed in fields that traditionally had been the preserve of foreigners in Switzerland.

Primary Sector

Foreigners did not represent a significant proportion of those employed in primary-sector occupations.[1] Nonetheless, some Italians worked in the small number of Swiss mines, and some foreigners worked in agricultural production.

Nearly half the number of people working as miners in Switzerland in 1910 was foreign.[2] According to Klaus Urner, only 107 Germans were employed in the mining industry,[3] so that the more than 2,000 foreigners were almost entirely of Italian origin. Mining in Switzerland has never been a major employer because of a scarcity of natural resources. What iron ore deposits were to be found had been mostly exploited by the end of the nineteenth century, and no coal was ever mined. By the first decade of the twentieth century, mining was limited, therefore, to extracting granite, lime, gravel, sand, marble, and slate. Mining these materials was accomplished only after elaborate infrastructure preparations. The mountainous landscape buried mineral reserves in regions difficult to reach. The most productive slate mines, for instance, were located in Elm, a village in the canton of Glarus, surrounded by mountains 3,000 meters high. Granite quarries in Ticino were accessible only after constructing the Gotthard railroad (1882). Their exploitation is said to have been "accomplished almost entirely with immigrant labor."[4]

In Swiss agriculture, foreigners from Germany, France, and Italy were employed, although in this field, too, Italians were the most numerous. There is some discrepancy about actual numbers of foreigners employed. The censuses of 1900 and 1910 listed approximately 13,000 foreigners. The *Schweizerische Statistik, Ergebnisse der eidgenössischen Betriebszählung* (Swiss statistic, results of the federal industrial census) of 9 August 1905, however, recorded somewhat higher figures.[5] The disparity between numbers may be explained by the different months of the year in which the counts were taken. Whereas population censuses were compiled from winter data, the 1905 business census was a summer count. The number employed in agriculture would have been larger during the summer, the peak period of production.

Foreigners employed in agriculture worked for the most part on farms in cantons bordering their regions of origin. Thus Germans were found mostly in Thurgau and Basel-Town, Italians in Grisons and Ticino, and French in Geneva. Germans were more often employed as farm owners, whereas Italians were more frequently employed as farm laborers.[6]

Although some foreigners were attracted to work in agriculture in Switzerland, nevertheless, the number was not significant. More foreigners chose other types of employment. How can the phenomenon be explained when a majority of migrants had been farmers or had grown up in rural families in their countries of origin? Two reasons may be suggested. Firstly, Swiss agriculture was not expanding, and therefore additional labor was not required. Secondly, foreigners migrating to Switzerland were attracted to better paid jobs in the manufacturing sector.

Agriculture in Switzerland, in accordance with agriculture in most European countries, was fundamentally transformed in the late nineteenth century as a result of increased imports of inexpensive grain from North America. Swiss agricultural production was realigned. Emphasis shifted to livestock products and away from grains and other crops. The shift in production meant that fewer farm laborers were needed for harvest and planting. From 557,739 employed in Swiss agriculture in 1880, the number had fallen to 477,118 by 1910.[7] This sector of the Swiss economy, therefore, was not recruiting foreign workers.

In other branches of the primary sector, namely, forestry and fishing, foreigners were similarly of minor importance. Those employed in forestry were nearly all Italians, with only approximately one hundred Germans.[8] Foreigners in forestry work were found predominantly in the mountainous canton of Grisons, which borders Lombardy in Italy.

Construction

Foreigners employed in construction work in Switzerland were predominantly Italian and almost exclusively male.[9] In some divisions of the industry, Italians outnumbered the Swiss. In the field of public works, which included railways, roads, bridges, elevated and underground structures, there were more than twice as many Italians as Swiss employed.[10] Similarly, the dominance of Italians in bricklaying in Switzerland was so extensive that the Swiss became hodcarriers for the skilled Italian bricklayers.[11]

Throughout the nineteenth century, foreign labor had been important in the construction industry. Foreigners played a major role in building Switzerland's railroads. Not only were Italians and Swabians largely responsible for the construction work, but German and French capital and English expertise were also used. At the beginning of the 1900s, by which time the principal railway lines had been completed, foreigners still comprised 90 percent of those employed.[12]

Switzerland was not a forerunner in railway history. Not until 1847 was the first Swiss railway opened, the Spanischbrötlibahn, which operated along the 22-kilometer stretch between Zurich and Baden. Previous to this, a French train from Alsace to Basel had reached Switzerland in 1844. The train connection between Germany and Switzerland was not in operation until 1855, when the Mannheim-to-Basel line was completed, and no rail line connected Switzerland to Italy until the construction of the Gotthard Tunnel in 1882.

The first stage of railway construction in Switzerland took place in the 1850s and 1860s amid the same kind of unplanned, contentious competition that marked railway construction in most countries of the world. However, the Swiss federal government had tried to avoid problems by commissioning two English engineers in 1849 to plan a national railway network. The English experts, Stephenson and Swinburne, submitted a report recommending a 650-kilometer plan consisting in the main of two national railway lines, one from Lake Geneva to Lake Constance and the other from Basel to Lucerne. Cities and cantons left out of the proposed network reacted strongly against the plan. Finally, the report was rejected under the pretext that "the Englishmen had not known the country and had not studied the local requirements."[13] As a result, the Swiss federal government was unable to control even the worst practices of the private railway companies until legislation was enacted in 1872, and not until 1898 were most railway lines nationalized.

Not only foreign labor and foreign experts, but also foreign capital were employed in constructing Swiss railroads. French capital supported one of the principal companies, the Centralbahn. German capital was used through the intermediary of the Swiss Credit Bank, set up in 1856. Seven and a half million Swiss francs from the Allgemeine Deutsche Creditanstalt of Leipzig provided half the original capital for the Swiss bank. The bank, in turn, supplied capital for constructing the Gotthard rail tunnel.[14]

Foreign workers carried out most of the construction work on the Gotthard tunnel, which was the first rail tunnel through the Swiss Alps. During the ten year construction period (1872 to 1882), thousands of Italians were employed. In Göschenen at the northern end of the nine-mile tunnel, there were 1,642 workers, and at Airolo at the southern end, there were 1,021. Altogether 177 workers were killed during the construction.[15] Mountain railways, such as the first cog railway built in Switzerland (1871) between Vitznau and Rigi-Staffel, were the work of Italians as well.

During the prewar period, the Simplon tunnel (1898 to 1906) was the major construction project undertaken by foreign labor. In the middle of the construction period (that is, 1901), on average 1,860 Italians were employed.[16] The tunnel, 12.25 miles in length, is still the longest railway tunnel in the world. It connects the Swiss town of Brig in the canton of Valais with Iselle, Piedmont, in northern Italy. A road wide enough for mule trains had long served as a route over the alps in this region. In the early 1800s, the road (Simplon Pass road) was widened by Napoleon's public works department. The railway tunnel, in contrast to the overland road, is much shorter in distance and not subject to closure because of snow.

Construction of the Simplon tunnel was of such superhuman proportions that it led Maxim Gorki to describe it in a collection of stories entitled *Fairy Tales from Reality*. Not only did construction workers spend eight hours a day underneath 3,553 meters of dark mountain "burrowing as moles," but flowing springs of hot water (130° F) also continually interrupted the construction work.[17]

We made a deep incision in the mountain and as we penetrated deeply into its interior, the earth prepared a very angry, unfriendly reception inside there. She breathed her hot air on us, so that our hearts faltered, our heads grew heavy and our limbs hurt. Many of us had this sensation. Then the earth slung stones and poured hot water over us. Indeed . . . it was frightful. Sometimes, when the fire burned as the water appeared completely red, my father said to me: "We have wounded the earth. She will drown us all, burning us with her blood." That was of course only talk, but when one hears such words deep in the earth . . . one easily forgets that it is only a product of fantasy.[17]

According to Foerster, one-third of the Italian workers on the Simplon tunnel came to Switzerland with their families.[19] The wages that they received were the motivation for coming, for they were "a little higher than those of North Italy."[20] A skilled mason, for instance, could earn six Swiss francs a day. The typical wage for unskilled laborers was less than three francs, however. Most of the Italians were in that category. This was the rate for an eight-hour day spent in underground construction or for a ten-hour day above ground.

During the two strikes, when the Swiss Army was called in, no one earned any wages. In 1899, soon after construction work began, and again in 1901, there were strikes by the work force. The work was especially dangerous, a fact reflected by the casualty figures. Altogether, during the eight years of construction, sixty workers lost their lives. During the first five months alone, "eight per cent had fallen sick or met with accident."[21]

Nonetheless, not all construction jobs performed by foreigners during the prewar period were equally strenuous. The experience of Pietro Bianchi, who first came to Switzerland at the age of fourteen as a *bocia* (assistant to a builder), was more representative.[22] He was recruited from his home village, Lenno on Lake Como in Lombardy, in 1898 by a local man who worked as a *paletta* (bricklayer) at Julius Honegger's textile factory in Wald, Zurich Oberland. The local agent, who is referred to as Benpecora by Bianchi, asked Bianchi's mother for permission to take him to Switzerland to work for nine months. After the job was over, Benpecora gave Bianchi's mother forty francs and retained three hundred Swiss francs for himself. The young man had worked twelve hours a day, six days a week for nine months. Bianchi explained that

> Benpecora had taken many boys with him to work as *bocia*. When he was at home during the winter, he looked for poor families in the village. The poorer the family, the better for him. He had never, however, taken his own son with him, for he had sent him to study.[23]

The next spring Bianchi went to work for Honegger in Switzerland again, but this time he went without Benpecora. He procured a passport for himself and worked as a plaster carrier, earning 2.50 Swiss francs a day. After spending three years at this factory, he worked as a mason for a builder, also in the town of Wald. This was summer employment, but during the winter, he worked for a builder in Lenno, Italy, his home town.

This pattern of employment was commonly followed by foreign workers in the construction industry because projects in Switzerland were often curtailed during inclement winter weather. "The coming of winter generally necessitates a reduction to a fourth or a sixth of the summer's contingent."[24] Nonetheless, several long-term projects continued year long. Workers on railway lines and bridges confronted high snows and severe frosts.[25] In 1905, Bianchi worked on the construction of the Ricken tunnel, which connected Uznach and Wattwil in nearby St. Gall canton. He settled in Zurich two years later, where he was employed as a construction worker, at first building the freight station for the Swiss Federal Railways.

Not all foreigners in the Swiss construction industry during the prewar period were from Italy. In the industrial census of 1905, 13,030 foreign workers from Germany were counted as well. They were employed mainly as skilled workmen, such as joiners, painters, carpenters, and fitters. In addition, a small proportion worked as proprietors of construction businesses[26] or as managers of large-scale construction projects. Arthur Bachem, a German immigrant who came to Switzerland with his family at the age of thirteen, was an example. He became director of construction of the Ricken tunnel.[27]

Services Sector

Although the tertiary sector as a whole was not so large an employer of foreign labor as the secondary sector,[28] nonetheless, in some branches, foreigners represented a significant proportion of the total work force. Especially in domestic service, commerce, and tourism, foreigners performed major roles. In health care, education, banking, and insurance, foreigners were also employed. In one service, culture and entertainment, foreigners comprised nearly half of those employed in Switzerland. Female foreigners played a larger role in the tertiary sector than in either the primary or secondary sectors. In three fields, domestic service, tourism, and education, female foreigners were more numerous than males.

Domestic Service

Employment as servants was the traditional way for women in the nineteenth and early twentieth centuries to earn a living. During the prewar decade, the field was the largest employer in Britain. In Switzerland in 1910, only agriculture and the textile industry employed more workers than domestic service.[29] It was the second largest field for foreign workers, who comprised 25 percent of all domestic servants.[30]

Foreign servants in Switzerland were mainly women from Germany.[31] The largest number came from Württemberg, followed by Bavaria, Baden, Alsace-Lorraine, and Prussia. According to Urner, almost half of all German women employed in Switzerland were to be found working as domestic servants.[32] Italian women were not so attractive to Swiss families as southern German women, whose language, food, and customs were similar to that of the German-speaking Swiss. "No household help was so prized as the German girls from neighboring regions."[33] German women came increasingly to Switzerland during the prewar period because of the scarcity of employment opportunities for women in southern Germany.[34]

COMMERCE

Switzerland attracted a large number of foreigners to work in retailing. Many nationalities were represented, male as well as female. It was in this field more than in any other that a foreigner had an opportunity to be self-employed. Out of every thousand foreigners employed in commerce in Switzerland in 1910, 28.6 percent were self-employed; 32.8 percent were employees (that is, administrative or clerical staff); 9 percent worked in a family business, and 38.6 percent were workers (that is, assistants).[35] The proportions contrast sharply to other fields in which foreigners were employed mainly as workers.[36]

Germans were the most numerous foreign nationality group in commerce, and the types of businesses in which they were engaged were very wide ranging.[37] They operated family jewelry, book, art, and music shops and owned or worked in department stores and credit businesses. In bazaars and the rag and secondhand trade, Germans were prominent. Traditionally important in manufacturing beer in Switzerland, they were also found in the beer retail trade.

Italians were also attracted to the retail business in Switzerland. According to Foerster, 5 percent of the entire trading population in Switzerland came from Italy.[38] They tended to set up shops where communities of Italian workers congregated. For instance, when construction workers were building the Gotthard tunnel, Italian "retail dealers settled about them."[38] Italian retailers were especially prevalent in Ticino and Grisons, as well as in Geneva and canton Vaud. Even in eastern Swiss cities, however, "the Italian tropical fruit hawker and chestnut vendor were a well-known sight on our streets."[39]

TOURISM

The Swiss tourist industry exerted a strong pull on foreigners. Not only were they employed as waitresses and chambermaids, but foreigners also started and owned restaurants and hotels and rented private rooms to lodgers. In a few cases, foreigners were responsible for establishing some of Switzerland's famous mountain resorts. This category of employment was not so clearly definable as other fields, for it has not been possible to separate restaurants and hotels used for business accommodation from those used for pleasure. Therefore, the description of the tourist industry used here is a broad one, including employment in all restaurants, hotels, inns, and boarding houses.

The emergence of Switzerland as a tourist center was not a rapid development. Throughout the nineteenth century, with the extension of railways and roads, previously inaccessible regions of Switzerland were developed for the alpinist, skier, and the medical patient. In the early nineteenth century, the French-speaking western parts of the country, centered in Geneva but extending to Lausanne and Vevey, were the most frequented tourist destinations. The Berner Oberland, with Interlaken as a center, and the Rigi region in Innerschweiz were the first two mountainous areas to attract tourists.

The English romantic poets did much to publicize Switzerland's attractions to the traveler. Wordsworth, as early as 1790, described a mountain journey he took over the alps along the Simplon Pass.

> When from the Vallais we had turned, and clomb
> Along the Simplon's steep and rugged road,
> Following a band of muleteers, we reached
> A halting place, where all together took
> Their noontide meal. . . .
> . . . After brief delay
> Crossing the unbridged stream, that road we took,
> And clomb with eagerness, till anxious fears
> Intruded, for we failed to overtake
> Our comrades gone before. By fortunate chance,
> While every moment added doubt to doubt,
> A peasant met us, from whose mouth we learned
> That to the spot which had perplexed us first
> We must descend, and there should find the road,
> Which in the stony channel of the stream
> Lay a few steps, and then along its banks;
> And, that our future course, all plain to sight,
> Was downwards, with the current of the stream.
> Loath to believe what we so grieved to hear,
> For still we had hopes that pointed to the clouds,

> We questioned him again, and yet again;
> But every word that from the peasant's lips
> Came in reply, translated by our feelings,
> Ended in this—that we crossed the Alps.[40]

Lord Byron, another English "foreign worker," stayed with the Shelleys in Geneva for several months in 1816. He wrote of Lake Geneva,

> Clear, placid Leman! thy contrasted lake,
> With the wild world I dwelt in, is a thing
> Which warns me with its stillness to forsake
> Earth's troubled waters for a purer spring.
> This quiet sail is as a noiseless wing
> To waft me from distraction; once I loved
> Torn ocean's roar, but thy soft murmuring
> Sounds sweet as if a sister's voice reproved,
> That I with stern delights should e'er have been so moved.[41]

It was not until the end of the nineteenth century that Switzerland was firmly established as a holiday center. The number of tourist facilities (hotels, restaurants, and inns) nearly doubled between 1894 and 1912.[42] Mountain resorts in Valais and Grisons were not important until the last quarter of the century. Ticino, the southern Italian-speaking canton, was the last to be developed as a tourist destination.

Foreigners were instrumental in creating Swiss resorts in the nineteenth century. It was a British alpinist who first scaled the Matterhorn in 1865. Interest in mountain climbing and winter sports facilitated development of resorts in Valais, especially Zermatt. Resorts in Grisons, in contrast to those in Valais, were first visited for health treatments. A German physician, Alex Spengler, founded a pulmonary sanatorium in Davos in the 1860s. Mineral baths at St. Moritz were developed in the 1850s, and a large spa hotel opened in 1860.[43]

During the period of extensive growth in Swiss tourism, foreign workers represented a substantial proportion of the work force—23.5 percent in 1910.[44] The majority was female and originated from Germany.[45] According to Urner, employment in the Swiss tourist industry attracted more German women than any other occupation with the exception of domestic service. German women worked as cooks, chambermaids, and waitresses or barmaids in Swiss inns, hotels, and restaurants. In addition, 6,700 foreign workers from Italy were also employed in Swiss tourist facilities.[46] A considerable number of foreign women operated boardinghouses or rented private rooms mainly in Zurich.[47]

Schlaepfer concluded that foreign workers were more often attracted to the restaurant side of the tourist business than to the hotel side. "Many foreigners were able to become independently employed relatively quickly by taking over or opening up a tavern or restaurant."[48] Foreigners employed in restaurants in Switzerland were mainly in the cantons of Zurich, Vaud, Geneva, Grisons, and Ticino.[49]

EDUCATION

Foreigners were also attracted to work in the teaching profession in Switzerland. In 1910, 9 percent of those employed in teaching were non-Swiss. They taught at all grade levels and were prevalent in the French-speaking region where they were employed mainly in private, secondary schools.[50]

Foreign female teachers were more numerous than foreign male teachers, particularly in French-speaking cantons and Ticino.[51] However, in two German-speaking cantons, namely, Zurich and Basel-Town, there were a larger number of foreign men in the profession than foreign women.[52]

In Zurich and Basel, a significant proportion of the university professors was foreign.[53] Moreover, "60 percent of the foreign professors in Switzerland were from Germany."[54] Braun argued that German professors at the universities of Zurich, Basel, and Bern were instrumental in propagandizing for the expansionist policies of Germany. They had jobs in universities, "which were key positions for the education of public opinion."[55]

During the quarter-century before the outbreak of World War I there was a large number of foreign students at the seven Swiss universities, as well. In 1907, for example, students from Russia represented 34.2 percent of all university students in Switzerland.[56] The number of female medical students from Russia was especially noteworthy.[57]

The significance of a large foreign presence at Swiss universities has not been extensively analyzed. However, in the early twentieth century, many people in Switzerland were strongly influenced by German, French, or Italian cultures. Foreigners at universities, whether students or professors, contributed to Swiss fears of foreign cultural domination.

CULTURE

Cultural work, which included employment in fine arts, theater, and music, attracted a very substantial number of foreigners. In 1910, 44 percent of the total number of people employed in cultural work in Switzerland were foreign.[58] The proportion of foreigners was even larger in music and theater, amounting to 77 percent of those employed in cultural performance.[59]

Foreign workers employed in music and theater before World War I were predominantly male.[60] However, the 427 foreign women employed represented 81 percent of the total number of female musicians and actresses in Switzerland.

In the early twentieth century, music and theater in Switzerland existed to a significant extent in only five urban centers—Zurich, Geneva, Basel, Bern, and Vaud (with Lausanne as the main city in Vaud).[61] Foreigners dominated the cultural scene slightly less in Geneva than elsewhere in Switzerland.[62] Nevertheless, there was a strong and frequently overwhelming cultural impact in both French- and German-speaking regions, which raised cultural identity problems for Switzerland. With foreign workers numerous in many economic fields and foreign culture widespread throughout the country, there were fears expressed that the country had become *überfremdet* (foreign dominated).

Health Care

Foreigners, both male and female, were important in this service industry, representing 18.5 percent of the total work force.[63] Women were more numerous than men, comprising 63.3 percent of all foreigners employed in health care in Switzerland in 1910.

Male foreign workers in health care were prevalent as dentists (26 percent of all dentists) and pharmacists (31 percent of all pharmacists), whereas foreign women worked as nurses. Female nurses from Germany were attracted especially to employment in mountain clinics in Grisons. Several German physicians had founded medical care centers in the Alps during the midnineteenth century. These hospitals and sanitoria continued during the prewar period to employ German foreign workers. By 1910, more than half the number of those employed in health care in Grisons was foreign born.[64]

Foreign employment in Swiss health institutions has also been a prominent feature of the post–World War II economy. During the 1960s in particular, the number of foreign women employed in health care in Switzerland doubled.[65]

8
CONCLUSION

Migration of foreign workers to Switzerland during the quarter-century preceding World War I played a significant part in the industrialization of the Swiss economy. The main purpose of this study has been to analyze the impact of this migration.

Two roles were formulated to categorize functions foreign workers performed in Swiss industry. They provided the labor force necessary to introduce mass production methods of manufacture (role 1). They provided one linkage in an interdependent regional industrialization process in central Europe (role 2). The two roles were not mutually exclusive, however. It has been demonstrated that foreigners frequently performed both roles in Swiss industry during the pre-1914 period. In some branches of Swiss industry, foreigners traditionally had been employed, whereas in other branches, foreigners were new to the labor force. They worked in Switzerland in a wide range of industrial jobs—as entrepreneurs, managers, technicians, self-employed artisans, skilled and unskilled laborers.

The first role described primarily the participation of Italian workers in Swiss industry. Foreigners were a supplementary factory labor force in those industrial branches undergoing a transition from craft manufacture to factory-based mass production. Since this transformation occurred during the quarter-century before World War I in many branches of Swiss industry, the large expansion in the number of foreigners in Switzerland could be viewed as part of the modernization of industry. Changes in manufacturing techniques usually entailed introducing new machinery, requiring a different type of work force. The number of foreigners employed in factories increased significantly between 1895 and 1911. Italian foreign workers were employed mainly in those factories where unskilled labor was required—in the manufacture of building materials, textiles, and food processing. Foreign workers from Germany were more numerous than Italians in factories requiring skilled labor, such as printing, wood processing, metalworking, and engineering. Foreign workers from France were significant in only watchmaking factories.

Foreign manpower was also instrumental in creating new factory-based branches of Swiss industry. During the pre–World War I period, a number of new manufacturing branches were established in Switzerland, namely, aluminum, several new food-processing products, chemicals, and electrical engineering. In the cases of these new industries, no traditional Swiss work force existed. Recruiting foreigners was an integral part of the growth in new branches.

In the case study of the textile industry (Chapter 5), the roles performed by foreigners in a traditional, partly declining industry were analyzed. It was concluded that foreign textile workers fit most closely into what has been identified as role 1. The transformation of several branches of textile manufacture from cottage to factory production took place with the employment of foreign workers. Changes in methods of textile production often included adopting new manufacturing equipment that required a work force other than the Swiss cottage worker. In the embroidery branch of the textile industry, it was demonstrated that introducing a particular machine (that is, Schiffchenstickmaschine) was responsible for the modernization process. Mass-produced embroideries were the leading textile export in Switzerland before the outbreak of World War I. Foreigners were recruited to work in embroidery factories to supplement Swiss cottage embroiderers. In the textile industry, foreign workers were mainly young women from Italy. The case study examined the impact of female migration on the growth of a Swiss industry.

The second role that migrants performed in the Swiss economy was their part in the interdependent industrial development of central European economic regions. This role applied primarily to German workers, for during the prewar period, there was substantial evidence of regionalization existing within an area comprising southern Germany and northern Switzerland. The migration of labor was seen not as an isolated population movement, but as one that reinforced other types of economic exchanges that took place within the industrial region. Technology was transferred, capital was invested, and trade was channeled to coordinate more fully the two countries' industries.

This role described the functions performed by foreigners in the Swiss engineering industry (Chapter 6). The interdependent growth of Swiss and German engineering branches involved a wide range of links between capital, management, and labor. Foreign workers were particularly important in transferring technology and developing industrial relations. Some Swiss engineering firms were more closely associated with Germany than were others. The types of linkages were analyzed in some detail in the study of the Swiss engineering firm Brown, Boveri & Co. It was found that capital, trade, and management were identified with Germany during the pre-1914 period.

The growth of two other Swiss industries, chemicals and printing, was shown to have been linked to the growth of corresponding German industries. The migration of labor provided one connection between Swiss and German chemical manufacture and between the printing trade in the two countries (Chapter 4).

Role 2 also described labor migration as a means of compensating for differences in the rates at which the two economies modernized. In several branches of Swiss industry, such as the manufacture of clothing, some types of food and wood processing, traditional manufacturing methods were maintained longer than in Germany. Migration from Germany to Switzerland, therefore, offered an alternative to structural unemployment for some German artisans. Carpenters, mechanics, foundrymen, tailors, brewers, and printers had moved between the two countries throughout the nineteenth century. During the pre-World War I period, the list of occupations expanded to include a wider range of German migrants.

The two roles played by foreigners in Swiss industry were described in the book within the overall framework of push-and-pull analysis. The motivations for a push out of Italy or Germany were juxtaposed to the attractions of the Swiss economy, which acted as the pull. In order to carry out the analysis, demographic features of the foreign population were examined (Chapter 2). It was found that the preponderance of foreigners who lived in Switzerland were both female and male, single, of prime working age; originated from southern Germany or northern Italy; and stayed in the German-speaking region of Switzerland for only a few years.

Moreover, to understand the push that encouraged foreigners to leave their countries of origin, it was necessary to gain some appreciation for economic and social conditions in southern Germany and northern Italy (Chapter 3). Southern Germans were pushed out of a rapidly industrializing economy in which agricultural and craftsmen jobs, in particular, were contracting. Political dissatisfaction, as well as economic difficulties caused by changes associated with modernization, were found to have created the push for the majority of southern German migrants. The number of German workers in Switzerland increased measurably during the early twentieth century. Although the economy in northern Italy expanded during the two decades preceding World War I, it was unable to absorb the increasing population. Faced with this problem, the Italian government encouraged its excess work force to leave the country. Switzerland, as well as several other European countries, became a destination for Italian workers.

However, it was not only the push out of Germany and Italy that provided the impetus for the large-scale movements of population. The expanding Swiss economy was an attractive pull. Chapter 1 described

Swiss geography and the state of the economy in the late nineteenth century. Chapter 4 examined eight branches of Swiss manufacturing, describing the types of roles that foreigners performed. Foreigners were attracted to factory work as well as employment as artisans in workshops. Chapters 5 and 6 described attractions of the textile and engineering branches of manufacture. Chapter 7 analyzed the pull to the nonmanufacturing sectors of the Swiss economy. It was shown that the largest number of foreigners worked in the Swiss construction industry and in Swiss households as domestic servants. During the prewar period, job opportunities in some Swiss services expanded. Employment in retailing, tourism, entertainment, education, and health care were attractive to foreigners. Foreign women were more prevalent in the tertiary than the secondary sector of the Swiss economy. Foreigners, however, were not attracted in large numbers to work in the primary sector. Swiss agriculture, as shown in Chapter 1, was contracting during this period and generating its own outward push of population.

The book analyzed one example of intra-European migration and its impact on the industrialization of one European country. The importance of immigration to the growth of the United States economy has been a topic of analysis by economic historians for many years. This book was one small attempt to begin a study of the significance of migration for the growth of European economies. The conclusions reached may have relevance for other countries. Not only did Italians and Germans work in other countries of Europe in addition to Switzerland, but other nationalities also moved within the Continent during the quarter century preceding World War I. Before population movements were restricted by war and postwar legislation, European industries were able to recruit labor throughout Europe.

Although migration of labor to Switzerland was the primary focus of the book, nevertheless it was found that population movements were frequently associated with other connections between economies. Capital, trade, technology, and management were found to have often moved in the same direction as labor. Sometimes the economic connections were so extensive that national boundaries lost some of their significance. Parts of two or more countries merged into a regional economy. In the case of Switzerland, evidence reinforced the concept of an industrial region consisting of northern Switzerland and southern Germany. In other parts of Europe, migration of labor may have also contributed to forming industrial regions.

NOTES

Introduction

1. Stephen Castles and Godula Kosack, *Immigrant Workers and Class Structure in Western Europe* (Oxford: Oxford University Press, 1973), p. 4. In 1969, they made up 0.9 percent of the population in Austria; in 1968, they were 7.1 percent of the population in Belgium; in 1969, they were 6.4 percent of the population in France; in 1970, they were 4.8 percent of the population in Germany; in 1967, they were 8.3 percent of the population in Luxembourg; in 1969, they were 2.2 percent of the population in Sweden; and at the end of 1969, they represented 16 percent of Switzerland's population.

2. Lucio Boscardin, *Die italienische Einwanderung in die Schweiz mit besonderer Berücksichtigung der Jahre 1946–1959* [Italian migration to Switzerland with special consideration of the years 1946–1959], ed. Edgar Salin and Gottfried Bombach, Staatswissenschaftliche Studien, Band 46 [Studies in political science, vol. 46] (Zurich: Polygraphischer Verlag, 1962), p. 90.

3. Eidgenössisches Statistisches Amt publications [Swiss statistical office publications], p. 96.

4. Kurt B. Mayer, "Postwar Migration to Switzerland," *International Migration* 3 (1965): 125.

5. *Eidgenössisches Statistisches Amt Publications*, p. 96. In 1880, there were 211,035 foreigners in Switzerland; in 1888, there were 229,650; in 1900, there were 383,424; in 1910, there were 552,011.

6. Studienkommission für das Problem der ausländischen Arbeitskräfte, *Das Problem der ausländischen Arbeitskräfte* [The problem of foreign workers] (Bern: Bundesamt für Industrie, Gewerbe und Arbeit, 1964), pp. 12, 18.

7. Herman-Michel Hagmann, *Les travailleurs étrangers, chance et tourment de la Suisse* [Foreign workers, fortune, and pain of Switzerland] (Lausanne: Payot, 1966), p. 22.

8. Hilde Wander, "Migration and the German Economy," in *Economics of International Migration*, ed. Brinley Thomas (Cambridge University Press, 1958), p. 197.

9. Ibid., p. 199.

10. *Eidgenössisches Statistisches Amt publications*, p. 96. In 1888, there were 112,342 Germans in Switzerland, and in 1910, there were 219,530.

11. Robert F. Foerster, *The Italian Emigration of Our Times* (Cambridge: Harvard University Press, 1919), p. 5.

12. Gianfausto Rosoli, ed., *Un secolo di emigrazione italiana: 1876–1976* [A century of Italian emigration 1876–1976] (Rome: Centro Studi Emigrazione, 1978), p. 19. During this period, 6,137,250 Italians migrated within Europe, and 7,894,360 emigrated overseas.

13. Foerster, *Italian Emigration*, p. 8. During the period 1906–10, the annual average number of emigrants from Italy to Austria-Hungary was 37,138; to France, 60,224; to Germany, 62,199; and to Switzerland, 77,305.

14. *Eidgenössisches Statistisches Amt publications*, p. 96. In 1910, there were 202,809 Italians living in Switzerland; in 1920, there were 134,628; in 1930, there were 127,093, and in 1941, only 96,018.

15. Rudolf Braun, *Sozio-kulturelle Probleme der Eingliederung italienischer Arbeitskräfte in der Schweiz* [Socialcultural problems of the incorporation of Italian workers in Switzerland] (Erlenbach-Zurich: Eugen Rentsch Verlag, 1970), p. 380.

16. *Eidgenössisches Statistisches Amt publications*, p. 313. In 1910, there were 59,126 foreigners employed in construction, and in 1970, there were 115,622 foreigners employed in construction in Switzerland.

17. Ibid., p. 96. In 1910, migration was 52 percent male, and in 1970, it was 56 percent male.

18. Ibid., p. 96.

19. Jean Golay, "Italian Labor in Switzerland," *Journal of International Affairs* 19, no. 2 (1965): 234.

Chapter 1. The Setting

1. Six of the cantons are half-cantons: Obwalden and Nidwalden; Basel-Town and Basel-Country; Appenzell Inner Rhoden and Appenzell Ausser Rhoden. In 1979, canton Jura became the twenty-third canton.

2. Oskar Bär, *Geographie der Schweiz* [Geography of Switzerland] (Zurich: Lehrmittelverlag, 1973), p. 99.

3. Ernst Schenker, *Die Sozialdemokratische Bewegung in der Schweiz von ihren Anfängen bis zur Gegenwart* [The social democratic movement in Switzerland from its beginnings to the present] (Bern, 1926), p. 6.

4. *Statistisches Jahrbuch der Schweiz 1891* [Statistical yearbook of Switzerland 1891], pp. 2–3. At the end of the nineteenth century, approximately one-quarter of the total land in Switzerland was unproductive, one-quarter was pasture and meadow, and one-quarter was woodland.

5. Wilhelm Bickel, *Bevölkerungsgeschichte und Bevölkerungspolitik der Schweiz* [Population history and politics of Switzerland] (Zurich: Büchergilde Güttenberg, 1947), p. 129.

6. Albert Hauser, *Schweizerische Wirtschafts-und Sozialgeschichte* [Swiss economic and social history] (Erlenbach-Zurich: Eugen Rentsch Verlag, 1961), p. 253.

7. Jost Krippendorf, "Tourism in Twentieth-Century Switzerland," in *Modern Switzerland*, ed. J. Murray Luck (Palo Alto, Calif.: Society for the Promotion of Science and Scholarship, 1978), p. 276.

8. Claude Zangger, "Energy Resources and Development," in *Modern Switzerland*, ed. J. Murray Luck (Palo Alto, Calif.: Society for the Promotion of Science and Scholarship, 1978), p. 64.

9. Département fédéral de l'Économie publique, *La Suisse économique et sociale, Première partie, exposé historique et systematique* [Economic and social Switzerland, first part, historical and systematic account] (Einsiedeln, Switzerland: Établissements Benziger et Cie., 1927), pp. 48–49.

10. *An Outline of the Development of the George Fischer Works* (Schaffhausen, Switzerland: George Fischer Ltd., 1950), p. 21.

11. Bär, *Geographie der Schweiz*, p. 77.

12. L. F. Haber, *The Chemical Industry 1900–1930* (Oxford: Clarendon Press, 1971), p. 161.

13. Jean-François Bergier, *Naissance et croissance de la Suisse industrielle* [Birth and growth of industrial Switzerland] (Bern: Francke Editions, 1974), pp. 132–33.

14. Kurt Mayer, *The Population of Switzerland* (New York: Columbia University Press, 1952), p. 166.

15. Ibid., p. 181.

16. Arbeitsgruppe für Geschichte der Arbeiterbewegung Zurich, *Schweizerische Arbeiterbewegung* [Swiss workers' movement] (Zurich: Limmat Verlag, 1975), p. 96.

17. Jürg Siegenthaler, "Zum Lebensstandard schweizerischer Arbeiter im 19. Jahrhundert," [On the living standard of Swiss workers in the nineteenth century] *Schweizerische Zeitschrift für Volkswirtschaft und Statistik* [Swiss journal for economy and statistics], December 1965, p. 434. He showed that the standard of living for the average worker fell between 1875 and 1885.

18. Francesco Kneschaurek, *Ein Jahrhundert schweizerischer Wirtschaftsentwicklung 1864–1964* [A century of Swiss economic development 1864–1964] (Bern, 1964), p. 139.

19. Bergier, *Naissance*, p. 120.

20. E. Bonjour, H. S. Offler, and G. R. Potter, *A Short History of Switzerland* (Oxford: Oxford University Press, 1952), p. 320.

21. Schweizerisches Zolldepartement, *Die Entwicklung des schweizern Aussenhandels 1886–1912* [The development of Swiss foreign trade 1886–1912].

22. Haber, *Chemical Industry, 1900–1930*, p. 163.

23. In 1898, the Swiss public accepted in a referendum a policy of railroad nationalization.

24. Hans von Greyerz, "Der Bundesstaat seit 1848," [The federal state since 1848] in *Handbuch der schweizer Geschichte*, Band 2 [Handbook of Swiss history, vol. 2] (Zurich: Verlag Berichthaus, 1977), p. 1076.

25. Dirk Hoerder, ed., *Labor Migration in the Atlantic Economies: The European and North American Working Classes during the Period of Industrialization* (Westport, Conn.: Greenwood Press, 1985). This book includes a section on migration in Europe before World War I.

26. Charlotte Erickson, ed., *Emigration from Europe 1815–1914, Selected Documents* (London: Adam and Charles Black, 1976), *passim*.

27. Wilbert E. Moore, *Economic Geography of Eastern and Southern Europe* (Geneva: League of Nations, 1945), p. 118.

28. Ibid., p. 119.

29. J. D. Gould, "European Intercontinental Emigration 1815–1914: Patterns and Causes," *Journal of European Economic History* 8 (Winter 1979). This is a review article.

30. J. D. Gould, "European International Emigration: The Role of Diffusion and Feedback," *Journal of European Economic History* 9 (Fall 1980): 291.

31. See Chapter 2 for a discussion of Swiss emigration.

32. Stephen Adler, *International Migration and Dependence* (Farnborough, England: Saxon House, 1977), p. 16. He quoted V. I. Lenin, *Capitalism and the Immigration of Workers*.

33. V. I. Lenin, *Imperialism, the Highest Stage of Capitalism* 1916, Reprint. (Moscow: Progress Publishers, 1978), p. 100.

34. Ibid.

35. Stephen Castles and Godula Kosack, *Immigrant Workers and Class Structure in Western Europe* (Oxford: Oxford University Press, 1973), pp. 6–7.

36. Delia Castelnuovo-Frigessi, *La condition immigrée, les ouvriers italien en Suisse* [The condition of immigrants, Italian workers in Switzerland] (Lausanne: Édition d'en Bas, 1978), p. 15. She quoted V. I. Lenin, *The Task of the Zimmerwald Left in the Social Democratic Party of Switzerland*.

37. Michael Piore, *Birds of Passage* (Cambridge: Cambridge University Press, 1979), p. 39.

38. Ibid., p. 35.

39. Julius Isaac, *Economics of Migration* (London: Kegan Paul, Trench, Trubner & Co., 1947), p. 215.

40. Ibid, p. 216.

41. Ibid.

42. Ibid., p. 217.

43. Ibid.

44. Brinley Thomas, "The Positive Contribution by Immigrants," in *U.S. Economic History, Selected Readings,* ed. H. N. Scheiber (New York: Knopf, 1964), p. 399.

45. The relationship between capital investment in Swiss industry and the employment of foreign workers is discussed in Chapter 4.

46. See Chapter 5.

47. Sidney Pollard, ed., *Region and Industrialisation, Studies of the Role of the Region in the Economic History of the Last Two Centuries* (Göttingen, FRG: Vandenhoeck and Ruprecht, 1980). Sidney Pollard, *Peaceful Conquest, the Industrialization of Europe, 1760–1970* (Oxford: Oxford University Press, 1981).

Chapter 2. Who Were the Foreign Workers?

1. Bickel, *Bevölkerungsgeschichte,* p. 166.

2. Jürg A. Hauser, "Demography and Population Problem," in *Modern Switzerland,* ed. J. Murray Luck (Palo Alto, Calif.: Society for the Promotion of Science and Scholarship, 1978), p. 4. Approximately 224,000 Swiss emigrated during this period.

3. Rudolf Schlaepfer, *Die Ausländerfrage in der Schweiz vor dem Ersten Weltkrieg* [Foreigner question in Switzerland before World War I] (Zurich: Juris Druck & Verlag, 1969), footnoote 47. In 1910, 54.2 percent of the foreigners in central European countries were male and 45.8 percent female, whereas in Luxembourg, the proportion was 60.8 percent male to 39.2 percent female.

4. Sex ratio of male to female was 0.996.

5. In 1900, there were 199,885 foreign males and 183,539 foreign females. In 1910, there were 285,180 foreign males and 266,831 foreign females.

6. In 1910, there were 104,198 males and 115,332 females from Germany; 118,103 males and 84,706 females from Italy; 28,842 males and 34,853 females from France; 19,783 males and 17,856 females from Austria-Hungary.

7. *Statistisches Jahrbuch der Schweiz 1904* [Statistical yearbook of Switzerland 1904], pp. 14–15. *Statistisches Jahrbuch der Schweiz 1915,* pp. 22–23. In 1900, there were 130,057 foreign single males and 112,418 foreign single females. In 1910, there were 182,916 foreign single males and 161,533 foreign single females.

8. Chapter 5 describes textiles, and Chapter 7 describes the service sector of the Swiss economy.

9. *Eidgenössische Volkszählung 1900* [Census 1900], 2 vols., 1: 382–83 and *Statistisches Jahrbuch der Schweiz 1915* [Statistical yearbook of Switzerland 1915], p. 23. In 1900, there were 51,486 male foreigners fourteen or under; 107,937 aged fifteen to thirty-nine; 33,238 aged forty to fifty-nine; 7,224 over sixty. In 1900,

there were 51,669 female foreigners fourteen or under; 92,837 aged fifteen to thirty-nine; 29,435 aged forty to fifty-nine; 9,598 over sixty. In 1910 there were 75,919 male foreigners fourteen or under; 151,393 aged fifteen to thirty-nine; 47,548 aged forty to fifty-nine; 10,320 over sixty. In 1910, there were 76,937 female foreigners fourteen or under; 133,877 aged fifteen to thirty-nine; 42,342 aged forty to fifty-nine; 13,675 over sixty.

10. *Eidgenössische Volkszählung 1910* [Census 1910], 2:22.

11. *Statistisches Jahrbuch der Schweiz 1919* [Statistical yearbook of Switzerland 1919], pp. 54–55. In 1910, there were 63,695 French, 219,530 Germans, 41,422 from Austria-Hungary, 202,809 Italians, and 26,972 from other countries.

12. Ibid. In 1870, there were 62,228 from France and 57,245 from Germany. In 1880, there were 53,653 from France and 95,262 from Germany.

13. Ibid. In 1930, there were 37,303 French in Switzerland. Not until 1970, when 55,841 French were counted, did the number of French in Switzerland increase.

14. Ibid. In 1910, 83 percent of the French in Switzerland lived in French-speaking cantons.

15. Ibid. In 1910, there were 75,887 from Baden, 57,091 from Württemberg, 30,373 from Prussia, 24,045 from Bavaria, and 32,134 from other areas.

16. This point is a major premise of the book and is discussed at length in Chapters 3, 4, and 6.

17. *Statistisches Jahrbuch der Schweiz 1919*, pp. 54–55. In 1900, there were 117,059, and in 1910, there were 202,800 Italians living in Switzerland.

18. Robert F. Foerster, *The Italian Emigration of Our Times* (Cambridge: Harvard University Press, 1919), p. 8.

19. Schlaepfer, *Die Ausländerfrage*, part 1, note 19.

20. *Statistisches Jahrbuch der Schweiz 1919*, pp. 54.

21. This is discussed in Chapters 3, 4, and 5.

22. *Statistisches Jahrbuch der Schweiz 1919*, pp. 54–55. In 1888, there were 14,181 Austrians; in 1900, there were 25,431, and in 1910, there were 41,422 living in Switzerland.

23. Hector Ammann, *Die Italiener in der Schweiz* [Italians in Switzerland] (Basel: Ernst Finckh Verlag, 1917).

24. Schlaepfer, *Die Ausländerfrage*, p. 70. He says that in the years before World War I, approximately 350,000 Austrians left the country, mainly as seasonal workers. From 1904, they went in increasing numbers to Switzerland.

25. Ibid., p. 71. By 1908, the number of Italian seasonal workers and the number of Italian temporary workers were equal—approximately 70,000 in each category. Schlaepfer took his data from de Michelis, who was Emigration Secretary in Geneva in the early 1900s.

26. In Chapter 4, there is a discussion of border crossers into Geneva watch factories and Basel chemical and silk ribbon factories.

27. Schlaepfer, *Die Ausländerfrage*, p. 180.

28. Ibid., p. 103.

29. Klaus Urner, *Die Deutschen in der Schweiz* [Germans in Switzerland] (Frauenfeld, Switzerland: Verlag Huber, 1976), p. 591.

30. Boscardin, *Die italienische Einwanderung*, p. 22.

31. Schlaepfer, *Die Ausländerfrage*, part 2, section 2, note 162. Out of 10,000 foreigners, 90 Austro-Hungarians, 88 French, 141 Russians, and 135 Americans became Swiss citizens from 1909 to 1913.

32. Ibid., p. 105.

33. The name of the law was Bundesgesetz betreffend die Erwerbung des

schweizer Bürgerrechtes und den Verzicht auf dasselbe [Federal law concerning the acquisition of Swiss citizenship and the renunciation thereof].

34. Ibid., p. 100.

35. German-speaking region: cantons of Zurich, Lucerne, Uri, Schwyz, Obwalden, Nidwalden, Glarus, Zug, Solothurn, Basel-Town, Basel-Country, Schaffhausen, Appenzell Ausser-Rhoden, Appenzell Inner-Rhoden, St. Gall, Aargau, Thurgau, and Bern. French-speaking region: cantons of Vaud, Neuchâtel, Geneva, Valais, and Fribourg.

36. Bickel, *Bevölkerungsgeschichte*, p. 168. There were 343,667 foreigners in the German-speaking region; 144,269 foreigners in the French-speaking region; 43,983 foreigners in Ticino; and 20,091 foreigners in Grisons.

37. Ibid., p. 167.

38. Ibid., pp. 135, 168.

39. Ibid., pp. 167–68. 40 percent of Geneva's population was foreign-born during the nineteenth century.

40. R. R. Palmer, *A History of the Modern World* (New York: Knopf, 1956), p. 563. In England in 1914, for instance, two-thirds of the population lived in places with 20,000 or more people.

41. Bickel, *Bevölkerungsgeschichte*, p. 144.

42. Ibid.

43. Mayer, *Population*, p. 256.

44. Wilhelm Bickel, *Die Volkswirtschaft der Schweiz, Entwicklung und Struktur* [Political economy of Switzerland, Development and Structure] (Aarau, Switzerland: Verlag Sauerländer, 1973), p. 206.

45. Ulrich Im Hof, *Geschichte der Schweiz* [History of Switzerland] (Stuttgart: Verlag Kohlhammer, 1974), p. 125.

46. Bickel, *Bevölkerungsgeschichte*, p. 167.

47. Jakob Lorenz, *Zur Italienerfrage in der Schweiz* [On the Italian question in Switzerland] (Zurich: Borsig, 1908), pp. 16–17.

48. Bickel, *Bevölkerungsgeschichte*, p. 167. *Eidgenössische Volkszählung 1900*, 1:327; *Statistisches Jahrbuch der Schweiz 1973*, p. 11. In 1888, 47 percent of all foreigners lived in Swiss cities; in 1900, 49 percent of all foreigners lived in cities and in 1910, 52 percent.

49. Mayer, *Population*, p. 203. The all-time annual maximum was in 1883 when 13,500 left Switzerland.

50. Jürg Hauser, "Demography and Population Problem," p. 4.

51. John Paul von Grueningen, *The Swiss in the United States* (Madison, Wisc.: Swiss-American Historical Society, 1940), p. 15.

52. Ibid., p. 19.

53. Ibid., p. 17.

54. Mayer, *Population*, p. 208.

55. Ibid., p. 211.

56. Ibid., p. 210.

57. Ibid., p. 208. Mayer reproduced the results of a study by Georges Lobsiger.

58. Ibid., p. 207.

59. Gerald Arlettaz, "Emigration et société" [Emigration and Society], *Schweizerische Zeitschrift für Geschichte* [Swiss journal for history] 31, no. 3 (1981):325.

60. Ibid., p. 330, note 23.

Chapter 3. Motivations for Migrating to Switzerland

1. *Statistisches Jahrbuch der Schweiz 1919*, p. 54.

2. Ibid.

3. Klaus J. Bade, *Vom Auswanderungsland zum Einwanderungsland? Deutschland 1880–1980* [From a country of emigration to a country of immigration? Germany 1880–1980], Peter Haungs and Eckhard Jesse, eds., Beiträge zur Zeitgeschichte, Band 12 [Contributions to modern history, vol. 12] (Berlin: Colloquium-Verlag Otto H. Hess, 1983), p. 24. Germans also emigrated overseas to Canada, Australia, Brazil, and Argentina.

4. Mack Walker, *Germany and the Emigration 1816–1885* (Cambridge: Harvard University Press, 1964), p. 176.

5. Bade, *Vom Auswanderungsland*, p. 25.

6. Jörg Schadt and Wolfgang Schmierer, *Die SPD in Baden-Württemberg und ihre Geschichte* [The Social Democrat party in Baden-Württemberg and its history] (Stuttgart: Verlag W. Kohlhammer, 1979), p. 19.

7. Zurich, the largest city in Switzerland before World War I, had 190,733 inhabitants.

8. Reinhold Grotz, *Entwicklung, Struktur und Dynamik der Industrie im Wirtschaftsraum Stuttgart* [Development, structure, and dynamics of industry in the economic region of Stuttgart] (Stuttgart: Geographische Institute, University of Stuttgart, 1971), p. 137.

9. Duisburg was the first.

10. Bernard Kirchgässner, "Der Aufstieg Mannheim als Bank-und Versicherungsplatz im deutschen Kaisserreich" [The rise of Mannheim as a banking and insurance place in the German Empire] in *Zur Geschichte der Industrialisierung in den sudwestdeutschen Städten* [On the history of industrialization of southwest German cities], eds. Erich Maschke and Jürgen Sydow (Mannheim: Jan Thorbecke Verlag Sigmaringen, 1977), p. 61.

11. Wolfgang Bocks, *Die Badische Fabrikinspektion, Arbeiterschutz, Arbeiterverhältnisse und Arbeiterbewegung in Baden 1879 bis 1914* [The Baden factory inspection, worker protection, worker conditions, and labor movement in Baden 1879 to 1914] (Freiburg/Munich: Verlag Karl Alber, 1978), p. 108.

12. David Blackbourn, *Class, Religion, and Local Politics in Wilhelmine Germany* (New Haven: Yale University Press, 1980), p. 77.

13. Klaus Urner, *Die Deutschen in der Schweiz* [Germans in Switzerland] (Frauenfeld, Switzerland: Verlag Huber, 1976), p. 267.

14. Susan Tegel, "Ludwig Frank and the German Social Democrats" (Ph.D. diss., London School of Economics, 1971), pp. 6, 71. She emphasizes the differences between north and south Germany, divided by the Main River.

15. Urner, *Die deutschen*, p. 610.

16. Erickson, ed. *Emigration*, document 4, p. 42, "Report on Laws and Customs affecting the Tenure of Land in the Kingdom of Württemberg" (Stuttgart, 20 November 1869) in "Reports from H. M. Representatives Respecting the Tenure of Land in the Several Countries of Europe" (British Parliamentary Papers, 1870) LXVII, pp. 83–86.

17. Hajo Holborn, *A History of Modern Germany 1840–1945* (New York: Knopf, 1969), p. 373. In Württemberg, one-third of the land was owned by peasants with less than five hectares of land. In Baden, two-fifths of the landholdings were smaller than five hectares.

18. Blackbourn, *Class*, p. 84.

19. Ibid., p. 85.

20. Landesarchivdirektion Baden-Württemberg, *Das Land Baden-Württemberg* [The Baden-Württemberg region] (Stuttgart: Verlag W. Kohlhammer, 1977), vol. 1, p. 624.

21. Blackbourn, *Class*, pp. 88–89.

22. *Statistisches Jahrbuch der Schweiz, 1910*, p. 41.

23. Urner, *Die Deutschen*, p. 445. Friedrich Merker, for example, arrived as a journeyman plumber, married in Rapperswil in 1839, and settled in Baden, Switzerland, where he started a household articles shop. Herman Greulich came to Switzerland in 1865 as a journeyman bookbinder and became a Swiss citizen in 1877.

24. Eugen Hermann, *Zürcher Quartierchronik* [Chronicles of the district of Zurich] (Zurich: Verlag Zürcher Quartierchronik, 1952), pp. 237–38.

25. Ibid., p. 46.

26. Ibid., pp. 244–45.

27. Robert Gellately, *The Politics of Economic Despair: Shopkeepers and German Politics 1890–1914* (Beverly Hills, Calif.: Sage Press, 1974), p. 32.

28. Blackbourn, *Class*, p. 144.

29. See Chapter 4 for further discussion of this point.

30. *Eidgenössische Volkszählung 1910* and *Fabrikstatistik des eidgenössischen Fabrikinspektorats 1911* [Factory statistics from the federal factory inspectors]. In 1910, 53,509 people worked in the wood-processing industry in Switzerland. Only 23,765 of these people worked in factories.

31. Urner, *Die Deutschen*, p. 341.

32. Blackbourn, *Class*, p. 149.

33. Bernhard Zeller, *Hermann Hesse in Selbstzeugnissen und Bilddokumenten* [Hermann Hesse in self-portrayal and picture documents] (Reinbek bei Hamburg: Rowolt Taschenbuch Verlag, 1963), p. 66. My translation of Hesse's writing.

34. Paul Burckhardt, *Geschichte der Stadt Basel* [History of the city of Basel] (Basel: Helbing & Lichtenhahn, 1942), p. 346.

35. *Statistisches Jahrbuch der Schweiz, 1919*, p. 54. In 1910, nearly one-third of all Germans from Baden who lived in Switzerland resided in Basel, namely, 23,532 out of 75,887.

36. See Chapter 4 for a more complete discussion of the chemical industry.

37. Bocks, *Die Badische Fabrikinspektion*, p. 482.

38. Martin Schaffner, *Die Basler Arbeiterbevölkerung im 19. Jahrhundert*, Band 123 [The Basel work force in the nineteenth century, vol. 123] Edgar Bonjour and Werner Kaegi, eds., Beiträge zur Geschichtswissenschaft [Contributions to historical knowledge] (Basel: Verlag von Helbing & Lichtenhahn, 1972), p. v.

39. Ibid., p. 26.

40. Urner, *Die Deutschen*, p. 451.

41. Heilwig Schomerus, *Die Arbeiter der Maschinenfabrik Esslingen* [The workers in the Esslingen machinery factory] (Stuttgart: Ernst Klett Verlag, 1977), pp. 75–77.

42. Schweizerisches Zolldepartement, *Die Entwicklung des schweizeren Aussenhandels 1886–1912*, pp. 286–87.

43. Ibid., p. 287. In 1892, 56 percent of all Swiss raw material exports went to Germany; in 1912, 55 percent. In 1892, 19 percent of all Swiss manufactured goods exports went to Germany; in 1912, also 19 percent.

44. Werner Näf, *Deutschland und die Schweiz* [Germany and Switzerland] (Bern: Verlag Herbert Lang, 1936), p. 53.

45. Werner Mittenzwei, *Exil in der Schweiz* [Exile in Switzerland] (Leipzig: Verlag Philipp Reclam jun., 1981), p. 17.

46. Ronald W. Clark, *Einstein, the Life and Times* (London: Hodder and Stoughton, 1973), p. 39.

47. Ibid., p. 40.

48. A. E. Senn and Alfred Erich, *The Russian Revolution in Switzerland 1914–17* (Madison: University of Wisconsin Press, 1971), pp. 3–9.

49. Urner, *Die Deutschen*, p. 724. Emil Hauth from Stafforth, Baden, was an example of the many who fled Germany to avoid military service. He arrived in Switzerland in 1892, became editor of a Swiss political newspaper, and left Switzerland for the last time during World War I.

50. Erich Gruner, *Die Arbeiter in der Schweiz im 19. Jahrhundert* [Workers in Switzerland in the nineteenth century] (Bern: Francke Verlag, 1968), p. 945.

51. Urner, *Die Deutschen*, p. 249.

52. Jorgen Schleimann, "The Life and Work of Willi Münzenberg," *Soviet Survey* (April 1965).

53. Schlaepfer, *Die Ausländerfrage*, part 1, note 19. In 1905, out of the 75,080 Italians entering Switzerland, 29,581 came from Lombardy, 16,660 from Venetia, and 12,508 from Piedmont.

54. Lorenzo del Panta, "Italy," in *European Demography and Economic Growth*, ed. W. R. Lee (London: Croom Helm, 1979), p. 230. He quoted Marrocchi's study. From 1876 to 1900, 56.8 percent of all Italian emigrants to Europe came from northeast Italy and 29.1 percent from northwest Italy. From 1901 to 1920, 44.1 percent came from northeast Italy and 30.6 percent from northwest Italy.

55. Foerster, *Italian Emigration*, p. 8. During the period from 1906 to 1910, the annual average number of emigrants from Italy to Austria-Hungary was 37,138; to France, 60,224; to Germany, 62,199; and to Switzerland, 77,305.

56. Rosoli, ed., *Un secolo*, p. 19. Forty-four percent of all Italian emigrants went to Europe (that is, 6,137,250), and 56 percent left the European continent (that is, 7,894,360).

57. Franco Amatori, "Entrepreneurial Typologies in the History of Industrial Italy (1880–1960): A Review Article," *Business History Review* (Autumn 1980):363.

58. Foerster, *Italian Emigration*, p. 125.

59. Hermann, *Zürcher quartierchronik*, pp. 50–51.

60. Foerster, *Italian Emigration*, p. 28. Data for return migration to Italy from European countries are incomplete. From Italian and Swiss census data, Foerster calculated return percentages of 65.6 percent (1888 to 1900) and 75.7 percent (1900 to 1910).

61. Enrico Serra, "Italian Emigration to France during Crispi's First Government (1887–1891)," *Journal of European Economic History* (Spring 1978):193.

62. del Panta, "Italy," p. 226. In northwestern Italy, the crude mortality rate was 27 per 1000 (1880 to 1883), and 19 per 1000 (1909 to 1913). In southern Italy, it was 32.6 per 1000 (1880 to 1883) and 22 per thousand (1909 to 1913).

63. Mayer, *Population*, p. 57. By 1910, the average crude death rate in Britain was 15.4, in Switzerland, 16.8, in Germany, 18.7, and in France, 19.4.

64. del Panta, "Italy," p. 205.

65. Mayer, *Population*, p. 75. By 1910, the average crude birth rate of Britain was 27.2; of Switzerland, 26.7; of Germany, 33.0; of France, 20.6; and of Italy, 32.2.

66. Ibid.

67. Alexander Gerschenkron, "Notes on the Rate of Industrial Growth in Italy 1881–1913," *Journal of Economic History* (December 1955):363. He divides

Italy's industrial growth into four periods, namely, 1881 to 1888, moderate growth; 1888 to 1896, stagnation; 1896 to 1908, very rapid; 1908 to 1913, reduced rate of growth.

68. Shepard Clough, *The Economic History of Modern Italy* (New York: Columbia University Press, 1964), p. 136.

69. Paul Bairoch, T. Deldycke, H. Gelders, and J. M. Limbor, *Working Population and Its Structures* (Brussels: Université Libre de Bruxelles, 1968), p. 106. The Italian population employed in agriculture in 1901 was 58.8 percent; in 1911, 55.4 percent; in.1921, 56.1 percent; in 1931, 46.8 percent.

70. Clough, *Economic History*, p. 152.

71. James Joll, *Europe since 1870* (Harmondsworth, England: Penguin Books, 1973), p. 124.

72. Arrigo Serpieri, *La guerra e le classi rurali italiane* [The war and the Italian rural class] (Bari, Italy: Gius Laterzo & Figli, 1930), p. 22. In Lombardy, 36.9 percent of the agricultural land was mountainous, and 49.5 percent consisted of plains; in Piedmont, 45.9 percent was mountainous and 23.2 percent plains; in Venetia, 30.2 percent was mountainous and 51 percent plains.

73. Foerster, *Italian Emigration*, p. 110.

74. Michele Morach, *Pietro Bianchi Maurer und Organisiert* [Pietro Bianchi bricklayer and organized] (Zurich: Limmat Verlag, 1979), p. 18.

75. Foerster, *Italian Emigration*, p. 121.

76. Clough, *Economic History*, p. 121.

77. del Panta, "Italy," 197.

78. Foerster, *Italian Emigration*, p. 125.

79. Volker Hunecke, *Arbeiterschaft und Industrielle Revolution in Mailand 1859–1892* [Working class and the industrial revolution in Milan 1859–1892] (Göttingen, FRG: Vandenhoek & Ruprecht, 1978), p. 74. The population of Milan in 1861 was 242,457, and in 1901 it was 491,460.

80. Clough, *Economic History*, p. 62.

81. Ibid., p. 95.

82. Hunecke, *Arbeiterschaft*, p. 100.

83. Ibid., p. 97.

84. *Statistisches Jahrbuch der Schweiz 1910*, pp. 102–13. According to the Swiss industrial census of 9 August 1905, there were 85,866 Italians employed in Swiss industry. Of this total, 65,092 were employed in construction and 3,783 in the metal and machine industries, predominantly male fields. The remaining 16,991 Italians were mainly women employed in Swiss industry.

85. Hunecke, *Arbeiterschaft*. p. 105.

86. Ibid., p. 120.

87. Ibid., p. 130.

88. Foerster. *Italian Emigration*, p. 474.

89. Serra, "Italian Emigration," p. 194.

90. Foerster, *Italian Emigration*, p. 474.

91. Boscardin, *Die italienische Einwanderung*, p. 15.

92. Foerster, *Italian Emigration*, p. 481.

93. Ibid., p. 495. Foerster quoted Enrico Corradini, *Il volere d'Italia* [The will of Italy].

94. Ibid. Foerster quoted Enrico Corradini, *L'ora di Tripoli* [The hour of Tripoli] (Milan: 1911).

95. Ibid,, p 500. Foerster mentions articles written by A. O. Olivetti beginning in 1911.

96. Charles P. Kindleberger, *Manias, Panics, and Crashes,* (London: Mac-

millan, 1978), pp. 134–35. He quoted Franco Bonelli, *La crisi del 1907: una tappa dello sviluppo industriale in Italia* [The crisis of 1907: a stopper of industrial development in Italy] (Turin: Fondzione Luigi Einaudi, 1971).

97. Moore, *Economic Geography*, p. 99.

98. Ibid., p. 119.

99. Ibid.

100. Richard A. Webster, *Industrial Imperialism in Italy 1908–1915* (Berkeley: University of California Press, 1975), pp. 126–63.

101. Ibid., p. 128.

102. Ibid.

103. Ibid.

104. Daniel L. Horowitz, *The Italian Labor Movement* (Cambridge: Harvard University Press, 1963), p. 30.

105. Joll. *Europe since 1870*, p. 124.

106. Morach, *Pietro Bianchi*, p. 21.

107. Horowitz, *Italian Labor*, p. 73.

108. Geoffrey Trease, *The Italian Story* (London: Macmillan, 1963), p. 283.

109. Clough, *Economic History*, p. 151.

110. Horowitz, *Italian Labor*, p. 78. In 1907, 575,630 workers took part in 2,268 strikes, including 1,891 industrial strikes with 321,499 workers involved and 377 agricultural strikes with 254,131 workers involved.

111. Ibid., p. 114.

112. Ibid., p. 113. There were 33,400 textile worker members, of whom 22,400 were women.

Chapter 4. Employment of Foreigners in Swiss Manufacturing

1. *Eidgenössisches Statistisches Amt publications*, [Swiss statistical office publications] p. 313. There were 179,444 foreigners employed in the secondary sector, of whom 59,048 worked in the construction industry. Since construction is not a manufacturing industry, discussion of the foreign impact on Swiss construction is analyzed in Chapter 7. There were 101,360 foreigners in the tertiary sector and 16,120 foreigners in the primary sector.

2. Bickel, *Bevölkerungsgeschichte*, p. 169.

3. Kneschaurek, *Ein Jahrhundert*, p. 139.

4. Ibid.

5. Bickel, *Bevölkerungsgeschichte*, p. 197.

6. *Eidgenössisches Statistisches Amt publications*, p. 313, and *Statistisches Jahrbuch der Schweiz 1923*, p. 116. In 1900, there were 83,078 foreign workers in Swiss manufacturing industries, of whom 40,068 worked in factories. In 1910, there were 120,318 foreign workers in Swiss manufacturing industries, of whom 73,333 worked in factories.

7. *Statistisches Jahrbuch der Schweiz 1896*, p. 126; *1902*, p. 100; *1913*, p. 113. In 1895, there were 14,872 Germans, 3,354 French, 5,124 Italians, and 1,896 Austrians employed in Swiss factories. In 1901, there were 18,375 Germans, 4,204 French, 14,028 Italians, and 3,063 Austrians. Whereas by 1911, there were 26,116 Germans, 5,973 French, 34,308 Italians, and 5,869 Austrians.

8. Lorenz, *Zur Italienerfrage*, p. 13. This remark by Sartorius von Walterhausen was quoted in the book.

9. *Statistisches Jahrbuch der Schweiz 1913*, p. 111.

10. Ibid. There were 3,331 French factory workers in Geneva in 1911, comprising 56 percent of the total number of French factory workers in Switzerland.

11. Ibid. There were 4,892 Italian factory workers in canton Zurich, 4,591 in canton St. Gall, 3,731 in Ticino, 3,715 in Thurgau, 2,365 in Geneva, 2,343 in Aargau, and 2,324 in Vaud.

12. *Statistisches Jahrbuch der Schweiz 1920*, p. 71. In 1910, 15 percent of the foreign workers were self-employed; 0.6 percent were executives; 5 percent were clerical staff; 62 percent were workers, and 18 percent were unskilled workers.

13. Ibid. In 1910, 31 percent of the Swiss were self-employed; 0.8 percent were executives; 7 percent were clerical staff; 55 percent were workers; and 8 percent were unskilled workers.

14. See Chapter 2 for a discussion of Swiss emigration.

15. *Eidgenössisches Statistisches Amt publications*, p. 313.

16. In Swiss factory statistics, the two manufacturing industries were grouped together before World War I.

17. *Eidgenössisches Statistisches Amt publications*, pp. 307, 313, 316.

18. Emma Steiger, *Geschichte der Frauenarbeit in Zurich* [History of women's work in Zurich] (Zurich: Statistisches Amt der Stadt Zurich, 1964), p. 185.

19. Bickel, *Die Volkswirtschaft*, p. 237.

20. *Statistisches Jahrbuch der Schweiz 1923*, p. 116, and *Eidgenössisches Statistisches Amt publications*, pp. 307, 313. There were 122,691 employed in clothing and shoes, of whom 24,850 worked in a factory.

21. Steiger, *Geschichte der Frauenarbeit*, pp. 194–195.

22. Ibid., *Die Arbeitsverhältnisse zürcherischer Ladentöchter und Arbeiterinnen* [Working conditions of shop girls and working women in Zurich]. Steiger reports on the results of this report, which was undertaken in 1914.

23. Ibid., p. 197. The average hourly rate paid for sewing women's and men's clothing was twenty-four rappen, whereas the hourly rate for plain needlework and household linen and underclothing was eighteen to twenty-one rappen. (One hundred rappens = one Swiss franc).

24. *Eidgenössische Volkszählung, 1910*, vol. 3, p. 100. There were 44,991 females employed in the manufacture of women's clothing, of whom 6,384 were foreign.

25. *Statistisches Jahrbuch der Schweiz 1920*, p. 71. 48 percent of the total number of foreigners employed in clothing production were self-employed.

26. *Eidgenössische Volkszählung, 1910*, vol. 3, p. 100. In Zurich, there were 3,691 tailors, of whom 1,805 were foreign in 1910. In Basel, there were 764 tailors, of whom 468 were foreign in 1910. In St. Gall, there were 970 tailors, of whom 455 were foreign in 1910.

27. Ibid. In Geneva, there were 1,185 tailors, of whom 747 were foreign in 1910. In Ticino, there were 714 tailors, of whom 384 were foreign in 1910.

28. Gruner, *Die Arbeiter*, p. 515.

29. Arbeitsgruppe für Geschichte, *Schweizerische Arbeiterbewegung*, p. 33.

30. Robyn Dasey, "Women's Work and the Family: Women Garment Workers in Berlin and Hamburg before the First World War," in *The German Family*, eds. Richard Evans and W. R. Lee (London: Croom Helm, 1981). Dasey describes the clothing industry in Germany.

31. Steiger, *Geschichte der Frauenarbeit*, p. 189.

32. See Chapter 3, part 1 for a discussion of motivations for emigration from Germany.

33. Urner, *Die Deutschen*, p. 446. Bally's grandfather migrated to Switzerland at the end of the eighteenth century.

34. *Bally 1851–1951*. Official company history.

35. Bickel, *Die Volkswirtschaft*, p. 218.

36. Hauser, *Schweizerische Wirtschafts*, p. 232.

37. Wolfgang Lehmann, *Die Entwicklung der Standorte der schweizerischen Industrien seit dem Ende des 19. Jahrhunderts* [The development of the location of Swiss industry since the end of the nineteenth century] (Zurich: Juris Verlag, 1952), p. 134. Wool and silk factories were usually larger in size, but textile factories averaged sixty-two workers per factory.

38. *Ergebnisse der eidgenössischen Betriebszählung 1905* [Results of the federal industrial census 1905], pp. 102–3. There were 17,617 Swiss employed in the shoe industry and 4,690 foreign workers, of whom 2,077 were German, 1,919 were Italian, 378 were Austrian, 242 were French, and 74 other nationalities.

39. *Eidgenössische Volkszählung 1910*, vol. 3, p. 101. In 1910, 23,924 were employed in the manufacture of shoes in Switzerland, of whom 5,702 were foreign.

40. Ibid. In canton Zurich, the industry was 34 percent foreign, and in canton Thurgau, it was 41 percent foreign.

41. Ibid. In canton Solothurn, there were 3,641 employed, of whom 1,586 were female Swiss workers, and only 196 were foreign workers. In canton Aargau, there were a total of 3,212 employed, of whom 1,159 were female Swiss workers, and only 228 were foreign workers.

42. Steiger, *Geschichte der Frauenarbeit*, p. 198.

43. E. Schiff, *Industrialization without National Patents* (Princeton: Princeton University Press, 1971), p. 110.

44. *Eidgenössisches Statistisches Amt publications*, pp. 313, 316. In 1910, there were 9,870 male foreign workers and 3,121 female foreign workers employed in the Swiss food-processing industry.

45. Ibid. and *Statistisches Jahrbuch der Schweiz 1913*, p. 116. In 1910, there were 55,902 employed in the Swiss food-processing industry, of whom 26,044 worked in factories.

46. Urner, *Die Deutschen*, pp. 446–47.

47. Ibid.

48. Ibid.

49. *Statistisches Jahrbuch der Schweiz 1913*, p. 113. In 1911, there were 3,193 Italians and 2,422 Germans working in Swiss food-processing factories.

50. Ibid., p. 112. In 1911, there were 26,044 employed in Swiss food-processing factories, of whom 12,604 were women.

51. *Eidgenössische Volkszählung 1910*, vol. 3, pp. 94–97. There were 6,019 employed, of whom 1,165 were foreign. The foreign workers included 544 males and 621 females.

52. Jean Heer, *The First Hundred Years of Nestlé 1866–1966*, p. 80.

53. Schweizerisches Zolldepartement, *Die Entwicklung*, p. 267.

54. Heer, *Nestlé*, p. 84. In 1898, Cailler opened a factory in Broc, Gruyere. Daniel Peter built a factory at Orbe in canton Vaud in 1901. Kohler moved into the Morges factory in 1898. Several chocolate companies became limited companies: Suchard in 1905, Peter in 1896, Kohler in 1898, Nestlé in 1875. Kohler and Peter merged in 1904 and were joined by Cailler in 1911. Nestlé and Anglo-Swiss merged in 1905.

55. Ibid., p. 80.

56. Foerster, *Italian Emigration*, p. 178.

57. Lorenz, *Zur Italienerfrage*, p. 10.

58. *Eidgenössische Volkszählung 1910*, vol. 3, p. 95. In Ticino, there were a total of 371 workers employed in the chocolate industry in 1910, of whom 226 were foreign (124 male, and 102 female). In Lucerne, there were a total of 321 employed, of whom 166 were foreign (48 males and 118 females).

59. Ibid., p. 99. In canton Aargau, there were 3,594 employed; in canton Vaud, there were 1,659 employed; and in canton Ticino, there were 1,559 employed.

60. Gruner, *Die Arbeiter*, p. 71.

61. Paul Haas, *Die tessinische Tabakindustrie und die Verhältnisse ihres Standortes* [The Ticino tobacco industry and the relationship to its location] (Bern: Verlag Dr. Gustav Grunau, 1930), p. 36.

62. *Eidgenössische Volkszählung 1910*, vol. 3, p. 99. There were 6,289 females and 2,838 males employed.

63. Ibid. In 1910, there were 3,594 working in tobacco processing in canton Aargau, of whom 225 were foreign. In canton Vaud, there were 1,659 working in tobacco processing, of whom 500 were foreign. In Ticino, there were 1,559 working in tobacco processing, of whom 576 were foreign.

64. *Eidgenössisches Statistisches Amt publications*, pp. 307, 313, and 316.

65. Burckhardt, *Geschichte*, passim.

66. George L. Huber and Karl Menzi, *The Story of Chemical Industry in Basle, CIBA* (Olten, Switzerland: Urs Graf Publishers, 1959), p. 111.

67. Hauser, *Schweizerische Wirtschafts*, p. 218 and CIBA publicity. Exports of chemical products in 1906 were valued at 7 million Swiss francs. In 1965, they were valued at 2.5 billion Swiss francs.

68. *Statistisches Jahrbuch der Schweiz 1913*, p. 113. In 1911, there were 1,189 Italian foreign workers and 1,145 German foreign workers employed in Swiss chemical factories.

69. L. F. Haber, *The Chemical Industry during the Nineteenth Century* (Oxford: Clarendon Press, 1958), p. 118.

70. Huber and Menzi, *Story of Chemical Industry*, p. 111.

71. *Schweizer Pioniere der Wirtschaft und Technik, (23). Alfred Kern, Georges Heberlein und Otto Keller* [Swiss Pioneers of economics and technology, Alfred Kern, Georges Heberlein, and Otto Keller] (Zurich: Verein für wirtschaftshistorische Studien).

72. Gustaf A. Wanner, *Fritz Hoffman-LaRoche 1868–1920, Zur Hundertsten Wiederkehr seines Geburtstages* [Fritz Hoffman-LaRoche 1868–1920, on the hundredth anniversary of his birth] (1968), pp. 31–32.

73. Haber, *Chemical Industry*, pp. 119–20.

74. Anonymous historical documents from Hoffman-LaRoche & Co., Basel. Patent protection was only one reason for Swiss chemical firms to locate in Germany. Easier access to the German market and German labor were other motives.

75. *Eidgenössisches Statistisches Amt publications*, pp. 307, 313, and 316.

76. Ibid., and *Statistisches Jahrbuch der Schweiz 1923*, p. 116. There were 53,509 employed in the Swiss wood-processing industry, of whom 23,765 worked in factories in 1911. In 1901, on the other hand, there were 50,971 employed, of whom only 14,381 worked in factories.

77. Schweizerisches Zolldepartement, *Die Entwicklung*, pp. 99–109. The value of exported flooring, joinery, and brushes rose significantly between 1886 and 1912. However, the value of exported raw timber for construction and boards fell because of rising home demand.

78. *Statistisches Jahrbuch der Schweiz 1891*, pp. 2–3.

79. G. de Michelis, "Arbeitslöhne in der Schweiz," [Wages in Switzerland], *Schweizerische Blätter für Wirtschafts und Sozialpolitik* [Swiss papers for economic and social politics], 17 (1909): 173–76.

80. *Eidgenössisches Statistisches Amt publications,* pp. 313. In 1900, there were 9,649 foreign workers, and in 1910, there were 12,056 foreign workers.

81. *Statistisches Jahrbuch der Schweiz 1913,* p. 113. In 1911, there were 3,795 Germans and 2,386 Italians employed in wood-processing factories.

82. Hermann, *Zürcher quartierchronik,* pp. 237–39.

83. *Eidgenössisches Statistisches Amt publications,* p. 313. In 1910 there were 4,483 foreigners employed in the industry.

84. See Chapter 3, part 1 for further discussion. Herman Greulich and Emil Hauth are examples from the prewar period.

85. Gruner, *Die Arbeiter,* p. 508.

86. Ibid., p. 509.

87. *Eidgenössische Volkszählung 1910,* vol. 3, p. 131. In Zurich, there were 2,380 employed, of whom 563 were foreign. In St. Gall, there were 693 employed, of whom 178 were foreign. In Basel, there were 768 employed, of whom 283 were foreign.

88. de Michelis, "Arbeitslöhne," pp. 173–76.

89. Urner, *Die Deutschen,* and E. Weckerle, *Herman Greulich. Ein Sohn des Volkes* [Herman Greulich. A son of the people] (Zurich, 1947), describe individuals who had significant political impact on Switzerland. The political role of foreign printers in Switzerland is not directly pertinent to this book.

90. George Fischer Works in Schaffhausen, described in Chapter 6, was a good example. Most engineering firms in Switzerland had their own foundries.

91. No accurate measure of output in this industry is available, since export statistics have been the measure used in this book. However, since engineering firms usually supplied their own cast materials, it can be assumed that when machinery exports rose, the output of the inputs increased accordingly.

92. *Eidgenössisches Statistisches Amt publications,* p. 313, and *Statistisches Jahrbuch der Schweiz 1923,* p. 116. In 1911, there were 41,142 employed in metalworking in Switzerland of whom 23,325 worked in factories. In 1911 there were 51,172 employed in engineering in Switzerland of whom 47,435 worked in factories.

93. *Statistisches Jahrbuch der Schweiz 1913,* p. 113. There were 9,180 foreigners employed in metalworking, of whom 6,218 worked in factories. Foreign workers in the metal-working industry comprised 22 percent of the total work force.

94. Schweizerisches Zolldepartement, *Die Entwicklung,* p. 95.

95. *Eidgenössische Volkszählung 1910,* vol. 3, p. 126. There were 575 employed, of whom 264 (46 percent) were foreign.

96. *Eidgenössisches Statistisches Amt publications,* p. 313, and *Statistisches Jahrbuch der Schweiz 1913,* p. 113. In 1910, there were 7,547 foreign workers in the Swiss building materials industry. In 1911, there were 6,125 Italians working in building materials factories. In this industry, the word *factory worker* refers to someone employed in a large-scale establishment.

97. Schweizerisches Zolldepartement, *Die Entwicklung,*pp. 113, 115.

98. *Eidgenössische Volkszählung 1910,* vol. 3, p. 104. In brick factories, there were 6,243 employed, of whom 2,163 were foreign. In cement works, there were 3,088 employed, of whom 1,371 were foreign. In limestone and plaster processing, there were 4,077 employed, of whom 1,768 were foreign.

99. *Eidgenössisches Statistisches Amt publications,* p. 316, and *Statistisches Jahrbuch der Schweiz 1923,* p. 116. In 1901, a total of 18,597 was employed, of whom 12,168 worked in a factory. In 1911, there were 18,824 employed, of whom 17,704 worked in a factory.

100. Bär, *Geographie,* p. 77.

101. David Landes, "Watchmaking: A Case Study in Enterprise and Change," *Business History Review* (Spring 1979), passim.

102. *Eidgenössisches Statistisches Amt* publications, p. 316, and *Statistisches Jahrbuch der Schweiz 1923*, p. 116. In 1888, there were 45,789 employed in watchmaking in Switzerland, of whom 12,394 worked in a factory. In 1901, there were 54,601 employed, of whom 24,858 worked in a factory. In 1911, there were 55,982 employed, of whom 34,983 worked in a factory.

103. Schweizerisches Zolldepartement, *Die Entwicklung*, p. 21. In 1888, the value of watch exports was 80,861 Swiss francs; in 1911, the value of watch exports was 164,027,00 Swiss francs.

104. *Eidgenössisches Statistisches Amt* publications, p. 313, and *Statistisches Jahrbuch der Schweiz 1913*, p. 113. In 1911, 4,071 foreigners worked in Swiss watchmaking, of whom 2,899 worked in factories.

105. Personal correspondence with Professor David Landes, Department of Economics, Harvard University, 13 April 1982.

106. Ibid.

107. Carlo Cipolla, *Clocks and Culture 1300–1700* (London: Collins, 1967), pp. 65, 70.

108. Ibid.

109. The business headquarters of watch companies remained in Geneva.

110. *Eidgenössische Volkszählung 1910*, vol. 3, p. 126. In canton Geneva, there were 2,435 employed, of whom 595 were foreign. In canton Bern, there were 21,832, of whom 1,237 were foreign. In canton Neuchâtel, there were 16,322 employed, of whom 1,239 were foreign.

Chapter 5. Foreigners in the Swiss Textile Industry

1. The textile industry includes cotton, silk, and specialized branches of these. The production of linen by the late nineteenth century was no longer significant, and wool manufacture was less significant than cotton and silk.

2. Walter Bodmer, "Der Einfluss der Refugianteneinwanderung von 1550–1700 auf die schweizerische Wirtschaft" [The influence of the migration of refugees from 1550–1700 on the Swiss economy], *Zeitschrift für schweizerische Geschichte* [Journal of Swiss history], no. 3 (1946).

3. Ibid., p. 18. The first refugees came to Geneva in 1542. By 1550, there were 127; in 1555, there were 380; and in 1559, there were 1,708. The total population of Geneva in 1543 was approximately 13,000.

4. Anton Largiarder, *Geschichte von Stadt und Landschaft Zurich* [History of the city and countryside of Zurich] (Erlenbach-Zurich: Eugen Rentsch Verlag, 1945). Locarno is located in the canton of Ticino, which became part of Switzerland in 1803.

5. Bodmer, "Der Einfluss," p. 57.

6. Walter Bodmer, *Schweizerische Industriegeschichte (Die Entwicklung der schweizerischen Textilwirtschaft im Rahmen der übrigen Industrien und Wirtschaftszweige)* [Swiss industrial history (The development of the Swiss textile economy in the framework of other industries and economic branches)] (Zurich: 1960), pp. 93–111.

7. The Edict of Nantes was a proclamation issued by the French king in 1598 granting religious freedom and civil rights to Protestants. Revocation in 1685 meant that Huguenots no longer enjoyed equal rights.

8. Warren C. Scoville, *The Persecution of Huguenots and French Economic Development 1680–1720* (Berkeley: University of California Press, 1960), pp. 126–27.

There were 3,000 to 4,000 Huguenots in Geneva, 2,000 in Bern, 4,000 to 8,000 in the Zurich area, and 6,000 in the canton of Vaud.

9. Ibid., p. 357.

10. Rudolf Braun, *Industrialisierung und Volksleben* [Industrialization and the life of the people] (Erlenbach-Zurich: Eugen Rentsch Verlag, 1960).

11. Rudolf Braun, *Sozialer und kultureller Wandel in einem landlichen Industriegebiet im 19. und 20. Jahrhundert* [Social and cultural change in a rural industrial region in the 19th and 20th centuries] (Erlenbach-Zurich: Eugen Rentsch Verlag, 1965), p. 11.

12. Hauser, *Schweizerische Wirtschafts,* p. 200.

13. Gruner, *Die Arbeiter,* p. 53.

14. Ibid.

15. Hauser, *Schweizerische Wirtschafts,* p. 201.

16. Gruner, *Die Arbeiter,* p. 55. There were 16,000 hand weavers and 14,193 factory-employed cotton weavers.

17. Ibid.

18. Hauser, *Schweizerische Wirtschafts,* pp. 201–2.

19. Haber, *The Chemical Industry,* p. 163. Measured in value, embroideries were the most valuable export (£8.4 million), followed by watches (£7.5 million) and silk goods (£5.6 million).

20. Gruner, *Die Arbeiter,* p. 59. In the 1840s, there were 15,000 silk ribbon weavers in Basel, of whom 1,500 worked in factories. In the 1860s, there were 22,000, of whom 4,921 were factory workers. In 1880, there were 18,000, of whom 5,005 worked in factories.

21. *Eidgenössisches Statistisches Amt publications,* [Federal statistical office publications], pp. 313, 316. In 1910, there were 26,947 foreign workers, of whom 19,005 were women.

22. Ibid. In 1900, there was 38,127 foreign workers in construction, and in 1910, there were 59,126.

23. Schaffner, *Die Basler Arbeiterbevölkerung,* p. 26. In 1888, of the total 4,632 employed in Basel's textile factories, 758 originated from Germany.

24. *Statistisches Jahrbuch der Schweiz 1913,* p. 113. In 1911, there were 20,611 foreign workers in Swiss textile factories, of whom 12,482 were Italian and 5,658 were German.

25. *Statistisches Jahrbuch der Schweiz 1896,* p. 126. *Statistisches Jahrbuch der Schweiz 1902,* p. 100. *Statistisches Jahrbuch der Schweiz 1913,* p. 113. In 1895, there were 91,454 workers in Swiss textile factories, of whom 6,892, or 8 percent, were foreign. In 1901, there were 97,193 employed in Swiss textile factories, of whom 11,632, or 12 percent, were foreign. In 1911, there were 100,175 employed in Swiss textile factories, of whom 20,611, or 21 percent, were foreign. In contrast, the number of Swiss workers in textile factories decreased from 84,562 in 1895 to 79,564 in 1911.

26. Ibid. In 1911, there were 4,622 foreign workers in Swiss cotton textile factories, representing 15.6 percent of the work force. In 1911, there were 5,977 foreign workers in Swiss silk textile factories, representing 19 percent of the work force. Whereas in the wool factories, there were only 1,727 foreign workers, or 32.4 percent, of the work force, and in linen factories, there were 280 foreign workers, representing 27.8 percent of the work force.

27. Ibid. In 1901, there were 2,740 German foreign workers and 1,384 Italian foreign workers in Swiss silk factories. In 1911, there was almost an equal number of Germans and Italians—2,761 Germans and 2,715 Italians.

28. Ibid. In 1901, there were 1,547 Germans and 1,673 Italian workers in

Swiss cotton textile factories. In 1911, there were only 800 Germans and 3,195 Italians employed in Swiss cotton textile factories.

29. Ibid. In 1901, there were 355 Germans and 465 Italians in Swiss wool factories. In 1911 there were 394 Germans and 1,214 Italian factory workers.

30. Alfred Bosshardt, Alfred Nydegger, Heinz Allenspach, *Die schweizerische Textilindustrie im internationalen Konkurrenzkampf* [The Swiss textile industry in international competition] (Zurich: Polygraphischer Verlag, 1959), p. 10. In 1911, the average number of workers in a Swiss textile factory was sixty-two. In wool-spinning factories, however, the average number of workers was 167; in silk factories, 145; and in cotton spinning, 118.

31. See Chapter 3, part 2 for discussion of this point.

32. Clough, *Economic History*, pp. 20–21.

33. *150 Jahre Rieter 1795–1945* [150 years of Rieter 1795–1945] (Winterthur-Töss, Switzerland: J. J. Rieter & Co., 1945), p. 78.

34. Albert Gasser, *Caspar Honegger*, Schweizer Pionere der Wirtshaft und Technik [Caspar Honegger, Swiss pioneer in the economy and technology] (Zurich: Verein für wirtschaftshistorische Studien, 1968), p. 59.

35. Bosshardt, Nydegger and, Allenspach, *Die schweizerische Textilindustrie*, p. 239. Tariff barriers on imported textiles were imposed by Germany in 1879, by the United States in 1883, by France in 1892, and by Russia in 1891.

36. Swiss exporters had difficulties during the American Civil War (1861 to 1865) when the U.S. market for Swiss silk goods was cut off. This may have been a major contributing factor to the growth of Swiss subsidiaries in the 1870s.

37. von Grueningen, *The Swiss*, p. 120.

38. Hansjörg Siegenthaler, "Switzerland in the Twentieth Century: The Economy," in *Modern Switzerland*, ed. J. Murray Luck (Palo Alto, Calif.: Society for the Promotion of Science and Scholarship, 1978), p. 94.

39. Bosshardt, Nydegger, and Allenspach, *Die schweizerische Textilindustrie*, p. 42. Although the Swiss textile industry as a whole was approximately 64 percent female during the period from 1895 to 1911, the silk branch was approximately 75 percent female.

40. *Eidgenössisches Statistisches Amt publications* [Federal statistical office publications], p. 310. The number of women in tourism rose from 29,515 to 39,272; the number of women in shopkeeping rose from 20,179 to 28,460; the number in health care rose from 6,548 to 10,571; the number in education rose from 10,663 to 14,018; and in transportation, from 3,614 to 5,377.

41. Marga Bührig and Anny Schmid-Affolter, *Die Frau in der Schweiz* [The woman in Switzerland] (Bern: Verlag Paul Haupt, 1969), p. 77.

42. Ibid., p. 73. In 1900, only 6.6 percent of the total number of employed women worked in offices.

43. *Statistisches Jahrbuch der Schweiz 1902*, p. 99, *Statistisches Jahrbuch der Schweiz 1913*, p. 112. In 1901, there were 48,360 women, and in 1911 there were 45,572 women employed in Swiss textile factories.

44. Bosshardt, Nydegger, and Allenspach, *Die schweizerische Textilindustrie*, pp. 212–13.

45. *Rüti 1824–1967, 125 Years Ruti Weaving Machinery* (Rüti, Switzerland: Rüti Machinery Works Ltd., 1967), p. 40.

46. *150 Jahre Rieter*, p. 248.

47. Bosshardt, Nydegger, and Allenspach, *Die schweizerische Texilindustrie*, p. 214.

48. Walter Ruegg, "Da kommt der Stoff her, der nach Freiheit riecht" [From

here comes the material that reeks of freedom], *Tages-Anzeiger* (Zurich), 15 September 1981, p. 11.

49. *Eidgenössische Volkszählung 1900* 1: 382–83. *Statistisches Jahrbuch der Schweiz 1915*, p. 23. In 1900, there were 20,243 foreign women aged fifteen to nineteen living in Switzerland, and in 1910, there were 30,388.

50. H. Wegmann, *Bericht über die Fabrikinspektion in der Schweiz, Kreis 1, 1912* [Report of the factory inspector of Switzerland, region 1 in 1912], p. 72.

51. H. Rauschenbach, *Bericht über die Fabrikinspektion in der Schweiz, Kreis 3, 1910–11* [Report of the factory inspector of Switzerland, region 3 in 1910–11], p. 213. These housing establishments or workers' hostels *(Arbeiterheime)* are described in more detail in the section on embroideries.

52. Schweizerisches Zolldepartement, *Die Entwicklung*, p. 63. *Statististique du Commerce 1921–24* [Statistics of commerce 1921–24], p. 19. The value of Swiss embroidery exports, measured in Swiss francs, was 77,521,000 in 1895. At the peak in 1919, the value of embroidery exports was 410,919,000 Swiss francs.

53. *Statistisches Jahrbuch der Schweiz 1913*, p. 113. In 1911, 25 percent of the work force in embroidery factories was foreign.

54. Georg Thürer, *St. Galler Geschichte, Aufklärung bis Gegenwart* [History of St. Gall from the enlightenment to the present] (St. Gall, Switzerland: Tschady Verlag, 1972), 2: 451–70. Approximately 100,000 people were employed in textiles, of whom 35,000 were in embroidery.

55. Bodmer, *Schweizerische Industriegeschichte*, p. 379.

56. Thürer, *St. Galler Geschichte*, p. 457.

57. Ibid.

58. Refer to notes 18 and 51 for Chapter 5.

59. Bodmer, *Schweizerische Industriegeschichte*, p. 383. In 1890, there were only 542 Schiffchenstickmaschine used in the Swiss embroidery industry. By 1900, there were 2,628 in use.

60. Ibid., p. 380.

61. Thürer, *St. Galler Geschichte*, p. 458. With the Schiffchenstickmaschine, one person could embroider 480,000 stitches in one day, compared with two people embroidering 40,000 stitches with a hand embroidery machine.

62. *150 Jahre Rieter*, pp. 137–38.

63. Thürer, *St. Galler Geschichte*, p. 458.

64. *Statistisches Jahrbuch der Schweiz 1923*, p. 116. In 1911, there were 28,606 workers in Swiss embroidery factories, and in 1923, there were only 13,866.

65. Elisabeth Gerter, *Die Sticker* [The embroiderer] (1938; reprint, Zurich: Unionsverlag, 1978), p. 173. (My translation.)

66. Thürer, *St. Galler Geschichte*, p. 460.

67. Bosshardt, Nydegger, and Allenspach, *Die schweizerische Textilindustrie*, p. 10. Embroidery factories had an average of fifty-four workers.

68. Ibid., p. 214.

69. *Statistisches Jahrbuch der Schweiz 1896*, p. 125; *1902, p. 99; 1913*, p. 112. In 1895, there were 13,336 factory embroidery workers, of whom 7,479 were women. In 1901, there were 16,751 factory-employed embroidery workers, of whom 10,191 were women. In 1911, there were 28,606 embroidery workers in factories, of whom 16,822 were women.

70. Wegmann, *Fabrikinspektion, Kreis, 1, 1910–11*, p. 53.

71. *Statistisches Jahrbuch der Schweiz 1913*, p. 112. In 1911, out of the total 7,580 minors employed, 5,337 were women.

72. Wegmann, *Fabrikinspektion Kreis 1, 1912–13*, p. 53.

73. Thürer, *St. Galler Geschichte*, p. 462.

74. Hauser, *Schweizerische Wirtschafts*, p. 344. The author quotes from school children's essays. An eleven-year-old Appenzell girl wrote that she embroidered six hours during school-term time and twelve hours during holidays. A twelve-year-old girl from Thurgau wrote that she spooled from 5:30 A.M. until 8:00 P.M. and then had free time.

75. Wegmann, *Fabrikinspektion, Kreis 1, 1912–13*, p. 53.

76. Ibid., 1910–11, pp. 54–55.

77. *Statistisches Jahrbuch der Schweiz 1913*, p. 113. In 1911, there were a total of 7,282 foreign workers in Swiss embroidery factories, of whom 1,463 were German, 4,717 were Italian, and 1,072 were from Austria-Hungary.

78. Lorenz, *Zur Italienerfrage*, p. 10.

79. Wegmann, *Fabrikinspektion, Kreis 1, 1910–11*, pp. 69–74. The following description of workers' hostels is mainly from Wegmann's description in factory inspection reports.

80. Ibid., p. 71.

81. One hundred rappen in Swiss currency equal one Swiss franc.

82. Rauschenbach, *Fabrikinspektion, Kreis 3, 1910–11*, p. 211.

83. Ibid., p. 199.

84. Mayer, *Population*, p. 181. Thurgau was 70.9 percent Protestant in 1888 and 63.4 percent in 1910. Appenzell Ausser-Rhoden was 91.6 percent Protestant in 1888 and 88 percent in 1910. St. Gall was 40.4 percent Protestant in 1888 and 38.3 percent in 1910.

85. Ibid. Zurich, Schaffhausen, Vaud, Basel, and Glarus became more Catholic.

86. According to the Swiss censuses of 1880 and 1910, the population of Thurgau was 7.5 percent foreign born in 1880 and 19 percent foreign born in 1910. In 1880, the canton had a total population of 99,231, of whom 7,432 were foreign. In 1910, Thurgau canton had a total population of 134,917, of whom 25,664 were foreign.

87. Studienkommission für das Problem der ausländischen Arbeitskräfte, *Das Problem*, p. 17. In 1910; 70 percent of the foreigners in Switzerland were Catholic, 26 percent were Protestant, 2 percent were Jewish, and 2 percent belonged to other religions.

88. *Statistisches Jahrbuch der Schweiz 1913*, p. 113. In 1911 in Thurgau, there were 18,714 factory workers, of whom 11,789 were Swiss, 3,715 were Italian, and 2,524 were German.

89. Ibid. In 1911 in Appenzell Ausser-Rhoden, there were 4,489 Swiss and only 266 Italians, 170 Germans, and 85 Austrians working in factories.

Chapter 6. Foreigners in the Swiss Engineering Industry

1. The official name for this industry used in the Swiss census is Maschinen, Apparate, Fahrzeuge [Machinery, apparatus, vehicles]. In this book, the term engineering will be used for this industry. In English, the word engineering includes branches that will be excluded from this chapter, namely, civil and industrial engineering. This chapter will use the word engineering in English to mean branches of mechanical and electrical engineering.

2. *Eidgenössische Volkszählung 1910*, 3: 127. There were 51,172 workers employed in iron foundries, machinery factories, and mechanical workshops, of whom 9,473 were foreign.

3. *Statistisches Jahrbuch der Schweiz 1923*, p. 116. There were 71,569 factory workers in the Swiss textile industry and 46,435 in the Swiss engineering industry.

4. Schweizerisches Zolldepartement, *Die Entwicklung*, pp. 9, 21. The value of textile exports in 1912 was 550,080,000 Swiss francs; the value of watch exports was 173,774,000 Swiss francs; and the value of machinery exports was 92,998,000 Swiss francs.

5. *Eidgenössische Volkszählung, 1910*, 3: 127. Eight cantons had more than 2,000 people employed in the engineering industry in 1910. These were the canton of Zurich, with 18,715; Aargau, with 5,268; Bern, with 4,862; St. Gall, with 2,972; Solothurn, with 2,926; Geneva, with 2,823; Schaffhausen, with 2,795; and Thurgau, with 2,491.

6. Hannes Hofmann, *Die Anfänge der Maschinenindustrie in der Deutschen Schweiz 1800–1875* [The beginnings of the machine industry in German-speaking Switzerland] (Zurich: Fretz & Wasmuth Verlag, 1962), p. 158. Rieter Machine Works in Winterthur, canton Zurich, was the only large engineering company that did not have a foundry at this time.

7. Département fédéral de l'Économie publique, *La Suisse économique*, pp. 48–49.

8. Gruner, *Die Arbeiter*, p. 68.

9. Hauser, *Schweizerische Wirtschafts*, p. 214.

10. By the turn of the century, this educational institution had become a leading scientific university in Europe. Technical colleges, such as the Technical College in Winterthur, were also established in the nineteenth century.

11. Hofmann, *Die Anfänge*, pp. 158–59.

12. *Statistisches Jahrbuch der Schweiz 1920*, p. 71. Statistics available from only 1910 listed 2,584 independently employed foreigners in the Swiss engineering and metalworking industries. Examples and reasons for this development are discussed in Chapter 3, part 1.

13. See Chapter 3, part 1. References are found in nineteenth-century literary, journalistic, and historical accounts.

14. Max Vuilleumier, "Von den Eisengiessereien im Kanton Zurich (1830 bis 1914)" [About the iron foundries in canton Zurich (1830 to 1914)] in *Beiträge zur Geschichte der schweizerischen Eisengiessereien* [Contributions to the history of Swiss iron foundries], eds. Hans Boesch and Karl Schib (Schaffhausen, Switzerland: Verlag der Eisenbibliothek Stiftung der Georg Fischer AG, 1960), p. 200.

15. Ernst Gehrig, "Zur Geschichte der Eisengiessereien im Berner und Solothurner Jura sowie im übrigen Kanton Solothurn 1800–1914" [On the history of iron foundries in the Bern and Solothurn Jura as well as in the rest of canton Solothurn 1800–1914], in *Beiträge*, p. 117.

16. The information about Sulzer Brothers comes from miscellaneous historical documents found in the Sulzer archives in Winterthur. The company's archive contains not only records of this company but also reports from the Swiss engineering industry in general.

17. H. Sitterding, ed., *Escher-Wyss 1805–1955* (Zurich, 1955), p. 15. This company has been owned by Sulzer since 1969.

18. Diesel was a workshop laboratory assistant. He corresponded with Sulzer engineers afterward.

19. *Statistisches Jahrbuch der Schweiz 1923*, p. 116, and *Eidgenössische Volkszählung 1900*. In the census of 1900, there were 35,090 people employed in the

engineering industry. According to Swiss factory statistics, in 1895, there were 23,921 workers in engineering factories, and in 1901, there were 32,647 workers in Swiss engineering factories.

20. *Statistisches Jahrbuch der Schweiz 1903*, pp. 102–3 and Vorort des schweizerischen Handels und Industrie Vereins, *Bericht über Handel und Industrie der Schweiz (Maschinen Industrie 1907–1913)* [Annual reports on trade and industry in Switzerland (engineering industry 1907–1913).

21. Urner, *Die Deutschen*, p. 457.

22. Information about this firm comes from their archive. Brown, Boveri & Co. has owned the company since 1967.

23. Adolf Wegmann, *Die wirtschaftliche Entwicklung der Maschinenfabrik Oerlikon 1863–1917* [The economic development of Maschinenfabrik Oerlikon 1863–1917] (Zurich: Müller, Werder & Co., 1920), p. 31.

24. Ibid., p. 80.

25. Sitterding, ed., *Escher-Wyss*, p. 6.

26. Ibid., pp. 80–81. In 1904, German companies that were members of the Zoelly syndicate were Siemens-Schuckert Werke, Friedr. Krupp (Germaniawerft), Vereinigte Maschinenfabrik Augsburg, Maschinenbaugesellschaft Nürnberg AG, and Norddeutsche Maschinen und Armaturenfabrik. The companies that joined the syndicate later were Schüchtermann & Kremer (Dortmund), Frat. Orlando e Comp. (Livorno), L. Lang (Budapest), Elsässische Maschinenbau-Gesellschaft (Mülhausen), Görlitzer Maschinenbau Anstalt (Görlitz), and Stork Brothers (Holland), Soc. Alsacienne de Constructions Mécaniques (France), and Soc. Nouvelle des Établissements Horme et Buira (France). In Britain, the following firms bought licenses to manufacture Zoelly turbines: Mather & Platt, John Musgrave & Sons, James Howden & Co. In the United States of America, the firm Cramp & Sons bought the license, and in Japan from 1917 to 1920, Ishikawashima and Mitsubishi manufactured Zoelly steam turbines.

27. Schweizerisches Zolldepartement, *Die Entwicklung*, p. 286.

28. Ibid., pp. 292–93.

29. *Statistisches Jahrbuch der Schweiz 1913*, pp. 112–13. In 1911, there were 46,435 factory workers in the Swiss engineering industry, of whom 7,867 were foreign born.

30. Vorort, *Bericht, 1907*, p. 135.

31. *150 Jahre Rieter 1795–1945* [150 Years of Rieter 1795–1945] (Winterthur-Töss, Switzerland: J. J. Rieter & Co., 1945), p. 166.

32. Heinrich Lotmar, "Die Lohn und Arbeitsverhältnisse in der Maschinenindustrie zu Winterthur" [Wages and working conditions in the engineering industry in Winterthur] *Zeitschrift für schweizerische Statistik* [Journal for Swiss statistics] (1907):4.

33. *Eidgenössische Volkszählung 1910*, 3:127.

34. Rudolf Vetterli, *Industriearbeit, Arbeiterbewusstsein und gewerkschaftliche Organisation* [Industrial work, workers' consciousness, and labor organization] (Göttingen, FRG: Vandenhoeck & Ruprecht, 1978), p. 125.

35. *Eidgenössische Volkszählung 1910*, 3:127. In the canton of Schaffhausen, there were 1,124 foreign workers in the engineering industry; in Geneva, there were 1,070; in Thurgau, there were 761; in Aargau, there were 657; and in St. Gall, there were 611.

36. Schweizerisches Zolldepartement, *Die Entwicklung*, p. 21, and *Statistisches Jahrbuch der Schweiz 1896*, p. 126; *1902*, p. 100; *1913*, pp. 112–13. In 1895, 202,640 machines were exported; in 1901, 307,402 machines; in 1911, 490,159 machines were exported. In 1895, there were 3,252 foreigner employed in Swiss engineer-

ing factories; in 1901, there were 4,860; and in 1911, there were 7,867 foreigners employed.

37. *Statistisches Jahrbuch der Schweiz 1902*, p. 100; *1913*, p. 113. Between 1901 and 1911, total employment in Swiss engineering factories rose from 32,647 to 46,435, or an increase of 13,788. During the same years, the number of foreign workers in Swiss engineering factories rose from 4,860 to 7,867, or an increase of 3,007.

38. Hermann Meyer, *Die Arbeiterbewegung in der schweizerische Maschinenindustrie im Jahre 1905* [The workers' movement in the Swiss engineering industry in the year 1905] (Zurich: Berichthaus Buchdruckerei, 1906), p. 31.

39. de Michelis, "Arbeitslöhne," p. 173–76. The variation depended on the region of Switzerland.

40. Siegenthaler, "Zum Lebensstandard," p. 432. In 1845, the wage rate was 2 Swiss francs per day; in 1855, it was 2.20; in 1865, it was 3.15; in 1875, it rose to 3.90. In the early 1900s, the daily rate was 5.20; in 1905, it was 5.40; in 1910, it was still 5.40; and in 1914, it had only increased to 5.80 Swiss francs per day.

41. Lotmar, "Die Lohn," p. 88.

42. Winterthur, Switzerland, Sulzer Brothers' archive papers.

43. *Erhebungen des schweizerischen Metallarbeiterverbandes* [Survey of the Swiss Metalworkers' Union Bern, 1910]. In Zurich from 1904 to 1909, rents rose 37.5 percent; in Baden, rents rose 26.3 percent; in Geneva, they rose 25 percent; and in Winterthur, also 25 percent.

44. Survey of the Swiss Typographical Union gave the average increase in the prices of milk, bread, and meat in twenty Swiss towns from 1900 to 1908.

45. Association for Historical Research in Economics, *Swiss Pioneers of Economics and Technology. The Peace Agreement* (Zurich: Verein fur wirtschaftshistorische Studien, 1967). Passim.

46. Meyer, *Die Arbeiterbewegung*, p. 30 (My translation.)

47. This trade union, which today is named Schweizerische Metall und Uhrenarbeiterverband (SMUV) [Swiss metal and watch workers' union], maintains an archive in Bern from which this data come.

48. Arnold Kamber, *Der schweizerische Metall und Uhrenarbeiterverband* [The Swiss metal and watch workers' union] (Bern: Unionsdruckerei, 1931), p. 66. In 1905, Swiss comprised 70.6 percent of the membership and Germans 19.4 percent. In 1909, Swiss comprised 74.5 percent of the members and Germans 16.5 percent. By 1914, Swiss represented 84.7 percent and Germans 8.6 percent.

49. See Chapter 3, part 1 for short biographies of these men.

50. *Volksrecht* (Zurich), 22–24 June; July 2, 18, 19, 23, 24, 26–28, 30 July; and 1 August.

51. The strike went into effect on 11 June when the period of notice ended. Altogether, two hundred men joined the strike at Rieter.

52. Arbeitgeberverband schweizerischer Maschinen und Metallindustrieller, *Jahresbericht 1910* [Annual report 1910], p. 27. Foundrymen at Sulzer Brothers and Swiss Locomotive Works had higher productivity.

53. Ibid., p. 29.

54. Ibid., p. 21.

55. Ibid., p. 29.

56. Ibid., pp. 22–23.

57. Data from Sulzer Brothers' archive. A total of 818 people worked at Sulzer's foundries in 1910.

58. Arbeitgeberverband, *Jahresbericht 1910*, p. 40.

59. Rieter Machine Works' annual report for 1910 to 1911. Winterthur, Switzerland.

60. Ibid. Foundry production from 1910 to 11 was 1,150,000 kilograms. This was 73,000 kilograms less than in 1909 to 1910.

61. Lotmar, "Die Lohn," p. 19.

62. Kamber, *Metall und Uhrenarbeiterverband*, p. 66.

63. The data come from a series of visits to Brown, Boveri & Co. archives in Baden and Oerlikon. I was given access to company annual reports, official histories, technical reports, lists of workers, and miscellaneous papers about working conditions. Maschinenfabrik Oerlikon became a member of BBC in 1967 and S.A. des Ateliers de Sécheron (a Geneva engineering company founded in 1879) became part of BBC in 1969. Today, the Swiss Group of BBC employs 20,000 people in eight factories in Switzerland.

64. He married the daughter of silk industrialist Conrad Baumann, who lent the 500,000 Swiss francs necessary to establish the firm.

65. Brown, Boveri & Co annual report 1911/12. Baden, Switzerland. Furthermore, in the annual report from the previous year, 1910–11, it was mentioned that Herr Hermann Röchling had joined the board of directors of BBC in Mannheim, "where we want to create a worthwhile connection with the German mining and iron industry."

66. C. E. L. Brown is listed in *Handelsregister* [business register] as originating from Brighton, England.

67. B. A. Behrend, "The Debt of Electrical Engineering to C. E. L. Brown," *Electrical World and Engineer* (1901): 10. The author discusses how unusual it was for a foreign firm to receive this contract.

68. Brown, Boveri & Co. annual reports from 1900–01 to 1914–15 listed members of the board.

69. Refer to the previous discussion of the German connection with this bank.

70. Miscellaneous archive paper from Brown, Boveri & Co.

71. Christian Müller, *Arbeiterbewegung und Unternehmerpolitik in der aufstrebenden Industriestadt, Baden nach der Gründung der Firma Brown Boveri 1891–1914* [Worker movement and entrepreneurial politics in a rising industrial city, Baden after the founding of the firm Brown Boveri 1891–1914] (Baden, Switzerland: Buchdruckerei Wanner AG, 1974), p. 83. In a quote from a contemporary newspaper in 1899, it was noted in passing that nine-tenths of the work force were Swiss citizens.

72. See Chapter 3 for a description of Fritz Merker.

73. *Eidgenössische Volkszählung 1888*, p. 110. There were 442 foreigners living in Baden in 1888, of whom eight spoke Italian.

74. *Eidgenössische Volkszählung 1900*, p. 114. There were 1,096 foreigners living in Baden in 1900, of whom 158 spoke Italian.

75. *Eidgenössische Volkszählung 1910*, p. 206. There were 1,768 foreigners living in Baden in 1910, of whom 260 spoke Italian.

76. Brown, Boveri & Co.'s annual report 1904–05 listed 1,172 workers and 168 employees at Brown Boveri Mannheim.

77. Brown, Boveri & Co.'s annual report 1907–08.

78. *50 Jahre Brown Boveri 1891–1941* [50 years Brown Boveri 1891–1941], Baden, Switzerland, p. 18.

Chapter 7. Foreigners in Nonmanufacturing Industries

1. *Eidgenössisches Statistisches Amt publications*, pp. 307, 310, 313, 316. In 1900, they comprised 3.4 percent of those employed in the primary sector, and in 1910, they comprised 3.5 percent.

2. Ibid. In 1910, there were 3,466 Swiss and 2,543 foreigners in Swiss mining.

3. Urner, *Die Deutschen*, p. 606.

4. Foerster, *Italian Emigration*, p. 174.

5. *Statistisches Jahrbuch der Schweiz 1910*, p. 41. In 1905, there were 9,862 Italians, 5,507 Germans, 5,101 French, and 1,128 of other nationalities employed on Swiss farms on 9 August.

6. Urner, *Die Deutschen*, p. 596.

7. Kneschaurek, *Ein Jahrhundert*, p. 139.

8. *Eidgenössisches Statistisches Amt publications*, pp. 307, 313. In 1910, 588 foreigners and 6,361 Swiss worked in forestry.

9. *Eidgenössisches Statistisches Amt publications*, pp. 307, 313, 316. In 1910, 46 percent of the construction workers in Switzerland were foreign.

10. *Statistisches Jahrbuch der Schweiz 1910*, pp. 104–5. In 1905, there were 20,904 Swiss and 45,321 Italians.

11. Foerster, *Italian Emigration*, p. 177.

12. *Eidgenössische Volkszählung 1910*, 3:107. In 1910, there were 12,095 railroad construction workers, of whom 10,879 were foreign.

13. Hauser, *Schweizerische Wirtschafts*, p. 289.

14. T. R. Fehrenbach, *The Gnomes of Zurich* (New York: McGraw-Hill, 1966), pp. 35–36.

15. Tobias Kästli, *Der Streik der Tunnelarbeiter am Gotthard 1875* [The strike of the Gotthard tunnel workers in 1875] (Basel: Z. Verlag, 1977).

16. Lorenz, *Zur Italienfrage*, p. 10.

17. Maxim Gorki, *Arbeit im Simplon* [Work in Simplon] (Zurich: Unionsverlag, 1977), pp. 7–9. This edition is extracted from Maxim Gorki, *Märchen der Wirklichkeit* [Fairytales from reality].

18. Ibid.

19. Foerster, *Italian Emigration*, p. 184.

20. Ibid., p. 183.

21. Ibid., p. 185.

22. Michele Morach, *Pietro Bianchi, Maurer und Organisiert* [Pietro Bianchi bricklayer and organized] (Zurich: Limmat Verlag, 1979).

23. Ibid., p. 30.

24. Foerster, *Italian Emigration*, p. 184.

25. Ibid., p. 176.

26. Urner, *Die Deutschen*, p. 603.

27. Ibid., p. 450.

28. *Eidgenössisches Statistisches Amt publications*, p. 313. In 1910, the tertiary sector employed 101,360 foreigners, and the secondary sector employed 179,444 foreigners.

29. Ibid., pp. 307, 313. In 1910, 457,707 worked in agriculture in Switzerland, 178,581 worked in textile production, and 138,575 worked as servants.

30. Ibid. In 1910, there were 59,126 foreigners employed in construction and 35,125 foreigners employed in domestic service.

31. Schlaepfer, *Die Ausländerfrage*, p. 28. The author says that two-thirds of the foreign servants came from Germany.

32. Urner, *Die Deutschen*, p. 609. He gives the figure as 46.6 percent.

33. Ibid., p. 610.

34. See Chapter 3, part 1 for discussion of this point.

35. *Statistisches Jahrbuch der Schweiz 1920*, p. 71.

36. Ibid. In Chapter 4, there is a discussion of the status of employed foreigners in manufacturing industries; 80 percent were workers.

37. Urner, *Die Deutschen,* p. 600.

38. Foerster, *Italian Emigration,* p. 179.

39. Ammann, *Die Italiener,* p. 30.

40. William Wordsworth, *The Prelude: Book VI* (1805), lines 562–66, 573–91, in *The Norton Anthology of English Literature,* vol. 2 (New York: W. W. Norton & Co. 1962), p. 153.

41. George Gordon, Lord Byron, *Childe Harold's Pilgrimage, Canto 3* (1816), lines 797–805, in *The Norton Anthology of English Literature,* vol. 2, p. 276.

42. Hubert Gölden, *Strukturwandlungen des schweizerischen Fremdenverkehrs 1890–1935* [Structural change of Swiss tourism 1890–1935] (Zurich, 1939), p. 234. In 1894, there were 5,209 establishments; in 1905, there were 7,686; and in 1912, there were 8,335.

43. Hauser, *Schweizerische Wirtschafts,* p. 297.

44. *Eidgenössisches Statistisches Amt publications,* pp. 307, 313, 316. In 1910, there were 7,992 foreign men and 10,416 foreign women employed in the Swiss tourist industry.

45. Urner, *Die Deutschen,* p. 610.

46. Foerster, *Italian Emigration,* p. 179.

47. *Eidgenössische Volkszählung 1910,* 3:134. There were 2,410 foreign women.

48. Schlaepfer, *Die Ausländerfrage,* p. 26.

49. *Eidgenössische Volkszählung 1910,* 3:134. In Zurich, there were 2,833 foreigners employed in restaurants, or 35 percent of the total employment. In canton Vaud, there were 2,060 foreigners, or 25 percent of the total number employed. In Geneva, there were 2,054 foreigners, representing 53 percent of those employed in restaurants. In Grisons, there were 1,554 foreigners, representing 32 percent of the employed; and in Ticino, there were 1,312 foreign workers in restaurants, representing 41 percent of the total number employed.

50. Ibid., p. 144. There were 24,747 teachers in Switzerland in 1910, of whom 2,225 were foreign. The largest number of foreign teachers were in the cantons of Vaud, with 359 teachers; Geneva, with 307; Zurich, with 290; Ticino, with 194; and Fribourg, with 193.

51. Ibid. In Vaud, there were 207 foreign female teachers and 152 foreign males. In Geneva, there were 211 foreign women and 96 foreign men. In Fribourg, there were 104 females and 89 males, and in Ticino, there were 116 females and 78 males.

52. Ibid. In Zurich, there were 181 foreign male teachers and 109 foreign female teachers, and in Basel, there were 57 foreign males and 43 foreign female teachers.

53. Rudolf Braun, *Sozio-kulturelle Probleme der Eingliederung italienischer Arbeitskräfte in der Schweiz* [The social and cultural problems of the incorporation of Italian workers in Switzerland] (Erlenbach-Zurich: Eugen Rentsch Verlag, 1970), p. 381.

54. Ibid.

55. Ibid.

56. Senn and Erich, *Switzerland 1914–1917,* p. 6.

57. Madelyn Holmes, "Go to Switzerland, Young Women, If You Want to Study Medicine," *Women's Studies International Forum* 7, no. 4(1984):243–45.

58. *Eidgenössische Volkszählung 1910,* 3:147. In 1910, there were 7,245 employed in cultural activities in Switzerland, of whom 3,198 were foreign.

59. Ibid., p. 149. In 1910, there were 2,264 employed in music and theater, of whom 1,743 were foreign. The number of male foreign workers in this field was 1,316, and the number of females was 427.

60. Ibid.

61. Ibid. Of the 2,264 employed in music and theater in Switzerland in 1910, Zurich employed 464, Geneva employed 379, Basel employed 287, Bern employed 276, Vaud employed 266, St. Gall employed 149, Grisons employed 126, Lucerne employed 93. Other cantons had fewer than 50 employed.

62. Ibid. In Geneva, 70.2 percent of those employed in music and theater were foreign, in comparison with the 77 percent for the whole country.

63. Ibid., p. 141. In 1910, there were 24,328 employed in health care in Switzerland, of whom 4,495 were foreign. There were 1,648 foreign men and 2,847 foreign women.

64. Ibid. In 1910, there were 852 employed in health care in the Grisons, of whom 436 were foreign.

65. *Eidgenössisches Statistisches Amt publications*, pp. 313, 316. In 1960, there were 11,634 foreign women employed in health care in Switzerland, and in 1970, there were 22,944. This represented in 1970 72.4 percent of the total number of foreign workers in health care.

BIBLIOGRAPHY

A. Primary Sources

Berichte über die Fabrikinspektion in der Schweiz. 1879–1913. (Reports of the Swiss federal factory inspectors.)

Eidgenössische Volkszählungen. 1888, 1900, 1910. (Recensement in French) (Censuses). Extracts from 1900 and 1910 censuses in *Eidgenössisches Statistisches Amt publications.* Bern.

Ergebnisse der eidgenössischen Betriebszählung 1905. Bern. (Results of the federal industrial census.)

Fabrikstatistik des eidgenössischen Fabrikinspektorats. 1895, 1901, 1911. (Factory statistics from the federal factory inspectors.)

Jahresberichte des Arbeitgeberverbandes schweizerischer Maschinen und Metallindustrieller. 1907–1912. (Annual reports of the Swiss engineering employers' association.)

Schweizerischer Metallarbeiterverband. Statistics from union's archive in Bern. (Swiss Metalworkers' Union.)

Schweizerisches Zolldepartement. *Die Entwicklung des schweizeren Aussenhandels 1886–1912.* (The development of Swiss Foreign trade 1886–1912.)

Statistisches Jahrbuch der Schweiz. 1891–1984. Bern: Statistische Bureau des eidg. Departements des Innern. (Statistical yearbook of Switzerland.)

Statistisches Jahrbuch für das Deutsche Reich. (Statistical yearbook of Germany). Berlin: Kaiserliches Statistisches Amt.

Vorort des schweizerischen Handels und Industrie Vereins, *Bericht über Handel und Industrie der Schweiz.* 1907–1913. (Annual reports on trade and industry in Switzerland by the central office of the Swiss Trade and Industry Association.)

Company Archives

Brown, Boveri & Co., Baden. Annual reports 1901–15, registers of workers, wage data, technical and biographical reports.

George Fischer Works (Eisenbibliothek)., Schaffhausen. Descriptions of social benefits, published company reports, and historical statistics.

Maschinenfabrik Oerlikon., Oerlikon. Annual reports 1901–15, miscellaneous historical documents.

J. J. Rieter., Winterthur. Annual reports 1906–14, published company histories.

Sulzer Brothers., Winterthur. Various biographical and historical documents, wage data.

B. Secondary Sources on Switzerland

Adams, Francis A., and Cunningham. *The Swiss Confederation*. London: Macmillan, 1889.

Ammann, Hector. *Die Italiener in der Schweiz*. Basel: Ernst Finckh Verlag, 1917.

Arbeitsgruppe für Geschichte der Arbeiterbewegung Zurich. *Schweizerische Arbeiterbewegung*. Zurich: Limmat Verlag, 1975.

Arlettaz, Gerald. "Émigration et société." *Schweizerische Zeitschrift für Geschichte* 31, no. 3 (1981).

Association for Historical Research in Economics. *Swiss Pioneers of Economics and Technology, The Peace Agreement*. Zurich: Verein für wirtschaftshistorische Studien, 1967.

Bär, Oskar. *Geographie der Schweiz*. Zurich: Lehrmittelverlag des Kantons Zurich, 1973.

Behrend, B. A. "The Debt of Electrical Engineering to C. E. L. Brown." *Electrical World and Engineer* (1901). Reprint from Brown, Boveri & Co.

Bergier, Jean François. *Naissance et croissance de la Suisse industrielle*. Bern: Francke Editions, 1974.

Bickel, Wilhelm. *Bevölkerungsgeschichte und Bevölkerungspolitik der Schweiz*. Zurich: Büchergilde Güttenberg, 1947.

———. *Die Volkswirtschaft der Schweiz, Entwicklung und Struktur*. Aarau, Switzerland: Verlag Sauerländer, 1973.

Biucchi, B. M. "Switzerland 1700–1914." In *The Fontana Economic History of Europe The Emergence of Industrial Societies, Part 2*, edited by Carlo Cipolla. Glasgow: Collins, 1973.

Bodmer, Walter. *Schweizerische Industriegeschichte (Die Entwicklung der schweizerischen Textilwirtschaft im Rahmen der übrigen Industrien und Wirtschaftszweige)*. Zurich, 1960.

———. "Der Einfluss der Refugianteneinwanderung von 1550–1700 auf die schweizerische Wirtschaft." *Zeitschrift für schweizerische Geschichte*, no. 3 (1946).

Boesch, Hans, and Schib, Karl, eds. *Beiträge zur Geschichte der schweizerischen Eisengiessereien*. Schaffhausen, Switzerland: Verlag der Eisenbibliothek, Stiftung der Georg Fischer AG, 1960.

Bonjour, Edgar; Offler, H. S.; and Potter, G. R. *A Short History of Switzerland*. Oxford: Oxford University Press, 1952.

Boscardin, Lucio. *Die italienische Einwanderung in die Schweiz mit besonderer Berücksichtigung der Jahre 1946–1959*. Staatswissenschaftliche Studien, Band 46. Zurich: Polygraphischer Verlag, 1962.

Bosshardt, Alfred; Nydegger, Alfred; and Allenspach, Heinz. *Die schweizerische Textilindustrie im internationalen Konkurrenzkampf*. Zurich: Polygraphischer Verlag, 1959.

Braun, Rudolf. *Industrialisierung und Volksleben*. Erlenbach-Zurich: Eugen Rentsch Verlag, 1960.

———. *Sozialer und kultureller Wandel in einem ländlichen Industriegebiet im 19. und 20. Jahrhundert*. Erlenbach-Zurich: Eugen Rentsch Verlag, 1965.

———. *Sozio-kulturelle Probleme der Eingliederung italienischer Arbeitskräfte in der Schweiz*. Erlenbach-Zurich: Eugen Rentsch Verlag, 1970.

Bührig, Marga, and Schmid-Affolter, Anny. *Die Frau in der Schweiz*. Bern: Verlag Paul Haupt, 1969.

Burckhardt, Paul. *Geschichte der Stadt Basel*. Basel: Helbing & Lichtenhahn, 1942.

Castelnuovo-Frigessi, Delia. *La condition immigrée, les ouvriers, italien en Suisse*. Lausanne: Édition d'en Bas, 1978.

Clerc, J.F. *Die Berufe der Maschinen und Metallindustrie*. Zurich: Rascher & Cie., 1924.

Département fédéral de l'Économie publique. *La Suisse économique et sociale, Première partie, Exposé historique et systematique*. Einsiedeln, Switzerland: Établissements Benziger & Cie., 1927.

Fehrenbach, T. R. *The Gnomes of Zurich*. New York: McGraw-Hill, 1966.

Foerster, Robert F. *The Italian Emigration of Our Times*. Cambridge: Harvard University Press, 1919.

Gasser, Albert. *Caspar Honegger, Schweizer Pionere der Wirtschaft und Technik*. Zurich: Verein für wirtschaftshistorische Studien, 1968.

Gerter, Elisabeth. *Die Sticker*. 1938. Reprint. Zurich: Unionsverlag, 1978.

Gilliard, Charles. *A History of Switzerland*. London: Allen & Unwin, 1955.

Golay, Jean. "Italian Labor in Switzerland." *Journal of International Affairs* 19, no. 2 (1965).

Gölden, Hubert. *Strukturwandlungen des schweizerischen Fremdenverkehrs 1890–1935*. Zurich, 1939.

Greyerz, Hans von. "Der Bundesstaat seit 1848." In *Handbuch der schweizer Geschichte*. Band 2. Zurich: Verlag Berichthaus, 1977.

Grimm, Robert. *Geschichte der Schweiz in ihren Klassenkämpfen*. 1920. Reprint. Zurich: Limmat Verlag, 1976.

Grueningen, John Paul von.*The Swiss in the United States*. Madison, Wis.: Swiss-American Historical Society, 1940.

Gruner, Erich. *Die Arbeiter in der Schweiz im 19. Jahrhundert*. Bern: Francke Verlag, 1968.

———. "Die Schweiz als Zentrum der Sozialdemokratischen Polnischen Emigration und die Beziehungen zwischen der Polnischen Exilfront in der Schweiz und der Polnischen Heimatfront 1880–1900." *Schweizerische Zeitschrift für Geschichte* 31, no. 1 (1981).

Haas, Paul. *Die tessinische Tabakindustrie und die Verhältnisse ihres Standortes*. Bern: Verlag Dr. Gustav Grunau, 1930.

Häsler, Alfred A. *The Lifeboat Is Full*. New York: Funk & Wagnalls, 1969.

Hagmann, Hermann-Michel. *Les travailleurs étrangers, Chance et tourment de la Suisse*. Lausanne: Payot, 1966.

———. "L'influence des étrangers sur l'évolution démographique de la Suisse." *Revue suisse d'économie politique et de statistique* 111, no. 4 (1975).

Hauser, Albert. *Schweizerische Wirtschafts und Sozialgeschichte*. Erlenbach-Zurich: Eugen Rentsch Verlag, 1961.

Heer, Jean. *The First Hundred Years of Nestlé 1866–1966*. 1966.

Hermann, Eugene. *Zürcher Quartierchronik*. Zurich: Verlag Zürcher Quartierchronik, 1952.

Hof, Ulrich Im. *Geschichte der Schweiz*. Stuttgart: Verlag Kohlhammer, 1974.

Hofmann, Hannes. *Die Anfänge der Maschinenindustrie in der Deutschen Schweiz 1800–1875.* Zurich: Fretz & Wasmuth Verlag, 1962.

Hottinger, M. *Geschichtliches aus der schweizerischen Metall und Maschinenindustrie.* Frauenfeld, Switzerland, 1921.

Hug, Lina, and Stead, Richard. *Switzerland.* London: T. Fisher Unwin, 1890.

Hughes, Christopher. *Switzerland.* London: Ernest Benn, 1975.

Ikle, Max. *Switzerland: An International Banking and Finance Center.* Zurich: Orell Füssli Verlag, 1970.

Jost, Hans Ulrich. *Links-radikalismus in der deutschen Schweiz 1914–1918.* Bern: Verlag Stampfli & Cie., 1973.

Kästli, Tobias. *Der Streik der Tunnelarbeiter am Gotthard 1875.* Basel: Z. Verlag, 1977.

Kamber, Arnold. *Der schweizerische Metall und Uhrenarbeiterverband.* Bern: Unionsdrückerei, 1931.

Kleinewefers, Henner, and Pfister, Regula. *Die schweizerische Volkswirtschaft.* Frauenfeld, Switzerland: Verlag Huber, 1977.

Kneschaurek, Francesco. *Ein Jahrhundert schweizerischer Wirtschaftsentwicklung 1864–1964.* Bern, 1964.

Krippendorf, Jost. "Tourism in Twentieth-Century Switzerland." In *Modern Switzerland,* edited by J. Murray Luck. Palo Alto, Calif.: Society for the Promotion of Science and Scholarship, 1978.

Landes, David. "Watchmaking: A Case Study in Enterprise and Change." *Business History Review* Spring (1979).

———. *Revolution in Time: Clocks and the Making of the Modern World.* Cambridge: Harvard University Press, 1983.

Largiader, Anton. *Geschichte von Stadt und Landschaft Zurich.* Erlenbach-Zurich: Eugen Rentsch Verlag, 1945.

Lehmann, Wolfgang. *Die Entwicklung der Standorte der schweizerischen Industrien seit dem Ende des 19. Jahrhunderts.* Zurich: Juris Verlag, 1952.

Lincke, B. *Die schweizerische Maschinen und Elektroindustrie.* Zurich, 1933.

Lorenz, Jakob. *Zur Italienerfrage in der Schweiz.* Zurich: Borsig, 1908.

Lotmar, Heinrich. "Die Lohn und Arbeitsverhältnisse in der Maschinenindustrie zu Winterthur." *Zeitschrift für schweizerische Statistik* (1907).

Luck, J. Murray, ed. *Modern Switzerland.* Palo Alto, Calif.: Society for the Promotion of Science and Scholarship, 1978.

Maillat, Denis, and Böhning, W. R. *The Economic Effects of the Employment of Foreign Workers: The Case of Switzerland.* Paris: OECD, 1974.

Matasar, Ann Sue. "Labor Transfer in Western Europe: The Problem of Italian Migrant Workers in Switzerland." Ph.D. diss., Columbia University, 1968.

Mayer, Kurt. *The Population of Switzerland.* New York: Columbia University Press, 1952.

———. "Intra-European Migration during the past Twenty Years." *International Migration Review* (1975):441–47.

———. "Postwar Migration to Switzerland." *International Migration Review* (1965):122–32.

Meyer, Hermann. *Die Arbeiterbewegung in der schweizerischen Maschinenindustrie im Jahre 1905.* Zurich: Berichthaus Buchdruckerei, 1906.

Michelis, G. de. "Arbeitslöhne in der Schweiz." *Schweizerische Blätter für Wirtschafts und Sozialpolitik* 17, no. 6 (1909).

Mittenzwei, Werner. *Exil in der Schweiz*. Leipzig: Verlag Philipp Reclam jun., 1981.

Morach, Michele. *Pietro Bianchi Maurer und Organisiert*. Zurich: Limmat Verlag, 1979.

Müller, Christian. *Arbeiterbewegung und Unternehmerpolitik in der aufstrebenden Industriestadt, Baden nach der Gründung der Firma Brown Boveri 1891–1914*. Baden, Switzerland: Buchdruckerei Wanner, AG, 1974.

Natan, Alex, ed. *Swiss Men of Letters*. London: Oswald Wolff, 1970.

Rey, Adolf. *Die Entwicklung der Industrie im Kanton Aargau*. Aargau, Switzerland, 1937.

Rubi, Fred. *Der Wintertourismus in der Schweiz, Entwicklung, Struktur und volkswirtschaftliche Bedeutung*. Basel: Arnaud Druck, 1953.

Schaffner, Martin. *Die Basler Arbeiterbevölkerung im 19. Jahrhundert*. Band 123. Basel: Verlag von Helbing & Lichtenhahn, 1972.

Schärer, Martin R. *Die Schweiz im 18. Jahrhundert*. Zurich: Verlag des Schweizerischen Landesmuseums, 1977.

Schenker, Ernst. *Die sozialdemokratische Bewegung in der Schweiz von ihren Anfängen bis zur Gegenwart*. Bern, 1926.

Schlaepfer, Rudolf. *Die Ausländerfrage in der Schweiz vor dem Ersten Weltkrieg*. Zurich: Juris Druck & Verlag, 1969.

Senn, A. E., and Erich, Alfred. *The Russian Revolution in Switzerland 1914–17*. Madison, Wis.: University of Wisconsin Press, 1971.

Siegenthaler, Hansjörg. "Switzerland 1920–1970." In *The Fontana Economic History of Europe, Contemporary Economies, part 2*, edited by Carlo Cipolla. Glasgow: Collins, 1976.

———. "Switzerland in the Twentieth Century: The Economy." In *Modern Switzerland*, edited by J. Murray Luck. Palo Alto, Calif.: Society for the Promotion of Science and Scholarship, 1978.

Siegenthaler, Jürg. "Zum Lebenstandard schweizerischer Arbeiter im 19. Jahrhundert." *Schweizerische Zeitschrift für Volkswirtschaft und Statistik* (December 1965).

Sitterding, H., ed. *Escher-Wyss 1805–1955*. Zurich, 1955.

Steiger, Emma. *Geschichte der Frauenarbeit in Zurich*. Zurich: Statistisches Amt der Stadt Zurich, 1964.

Steinberg, Jonathan. *Why Switzerland*. Cambridge: Cambridge University Press, 1976.

Studienkommission für das Problem der ausländischen Arbeitskräfte. *Das Problem der ausländischen Arbeitskräfte*. Bern: Bundesamt für Industrie, Gewerbe und Arbeit, 1964.

Swiss Office for the Development of Trade. *Economic and Industrial Switzerland*. Lausanne, 1928.

Thürer, Georg. *St. Galler Geschichte, Aufklärung bis Gegenwart*. St. Gall, Switzerland: Tschady Verlag, 1972.

Trachsel, Peter. *Der Einsatz italienischer Arbeitskräfte in der schweizerischen Landwirtschaft*. Winterthur, Switzerland: Verlag P. G. Keller, 1958.

Urner, Klaus. *Die Deutschen in der Schweiz*. Frauenfeld, Switzerland: Verlag Huber, 1976.

Vetterli, Rudolf. *Industriearbeit, Arbeiterbewusstein und gewerkschaftliche Organisation*. Göttingen, FRG: Vandenhoeck & Ruprecht, 1978.

Volksrecht. Zurich daily newspaper, June, July, August 1910.

Wanner, Gustaf A. *Fritz Hoffmann-LaRoche 1868–1920, Zur Hundersten Wiederkehrseines Geburtstages*. Basel, 1968.

Wegmann, Adolf. *Die wirtschaftliche Entwicklung der Maschinenfabrik Oerlikon 1863–1917*. Zurich: Müller, Werder & Co., 1920.

Ziegler, Jean. *Eine Schweiz über jeden Verdacht erhaben*. Darmstadt, FRG: Hermann Luchterhand Verlag, 1976.

COMPANY HISTORIES

Bally, Schönenwerd.

Brown, Boveri & Co., Baden.

CIBA, Basel.

Escher Wyss, Zurich.

George Fischer, Schaffhausen.

Hoffmann-LaRoche, Basel.

Nestlé, Vevey.

J. J. Rieter & Co., Winterthur.

Rüti Machinery Works, Rüti.

Sandoz, Basel.

Saurer, Arbon.

Schweizerische Kreditanstalt, Zurich.

Schweizerische Lokomotiv und Maschinenfabrik, Winterthur.

Sulzer Brothers, Winterthur.

C. General Secondary Sources

Adler, Stephen. *International Migration and Dependence*. Farnborough, England: Saxon House, 1977.

Amatori, Franco. "Entrepreneurial Typologies in the History of Industrial Italy (1880–1960): A Review Article." *Business History Review* (Autumn 1980).

Bade, Klaus J. *Vom Auswanderungsland zum Einwanderungsland? Deutschland 1880–1980*. Berlin: Colloquium-Verlag Otto H. Hess, 1983.

Bairoch, Paul; Deldycke, T; Gelders, H.; and Limbor, J. M. *Working Population and Its Structure*. Brussels: Université Libre de Bruxelles, 1968.

Berger, John. *The Seventh Man*. Harmondsworth, England: Penguin Books, 1977.

Blackbourn, David. *Class, Religion, and Local Politics in Wilhelmine Germany*. New Haven: Yale University Press, 1980.

Bocks, Wolfgang. *Die Badische Fabrikinspection, Arbeiterschutz, Arbeiterverhältnisse und Arbeiterbewegung in Baden 1879 bis 1914*. Freiburg/Munich: Verlag Karl Alber, 1978.

Borscheid, Peter. *Textilarbeiterschaft in der Industrialisierung. Soziale Lage versus Mobilität in Württemberg 19, Jahrhundert*. Stuttgart: Klett-Cotta, 1978.

Bosworth, R. J. B. *Italy, the Least of the Great Powers: Italian Foreign Policy before the First World War.* Cambridge: Cambridge University Press, 1979.

Brabazon, James. *Albert Schweitzer.* London: Gollancz, 1976.

Byron, Lord (Gordon, George). *Childe Harold's Pilgrimage, Canto 3* (1816). In *The Norton Anthology of English Literature.* Vol. 2. New York: W. W. Norton & Co., 1962.

Castles, Stephen, and Kosack, Godula. *Immigrant Workers and Class Structure in Western Europe.* Oxford: Oxford University Press, 1973.

————. *Here for Good.* London: Pluto Press, 1984.

Church, Roy A. "Nineteenth-Century Clock Technology in Britain, the United States, and Switzerland." *Economic History Review,* 2d series, 28 (1975):616–30.

Cipolla, Carlo. *Clocks and Culture 1300–1700.* London: Collins, 1967.

Clark, Ronald W. *Einstein, The Life and Times.* London: Hodder and Stoughton, 1973.

Clough, Shepard. *The Economic History of Modern Italy.* New York: Columbia University Press, 1964.

Cohen, Jon S. *Finance and Industrialization in Italy 1894–1914.* New York: Arno Press, 1977.

Coleman, Donald Cuthbert. *Courtaulds, an Economic and Social History.* Oxford: Oxford University Press, 1969.

Crowther, James Gerald. *Six Great Engineers.* London: Hamish Hamilton, 1959.

Engels, Friedrich. *Revolution and Counterrevolution in Germany.* Edited by L. Krieger. Chicago: University of Chicago Press, 1967.

Erickson, Charlotte, ed. *Emigration from Europe 1815–1914, Selected Documents.* London: Adam and Charles Black, 1976.

Evans, Richard., ed. *Society and Politics in Wilhelmine Germany.* London: Croom Helm, 1978.

Evans, Richard, and Lee, W., eds. *The German Family.* London: Croom Helm, 1981.

Gellately, Robert. *The Politics of Economic Despair: Shopkeepers and German Politics 1890–1914.* Beverly Hills, Calif.: Sage Press, 1974.

Gerschenkron, Alexander. "Notes on the Rate of Industrial Growth in Italy 1881–1913." *Journal of Economic History* (December 1955).

Gönner, Eberhard and Haselier, Günther. *Baden-Württemberg, Geschichte seiner Länder und Territorien.* Würzburg: Verlag Ploetz, 1975.

Gorki, Maxim. "Arbeit im Simplon." *Märchen der Wirklichkeit.* Reprint. Zurich: Unionsverlag, 1977.

Gould, J. D. "European Intercontinental Emigration 1815–1914: Patterns and Causes." *Journal of European Economic History* 9 (Winter 1979).

————. "European International Emigration: The Role of Diffusion and Feedback." *Journal of European Economic History* 9 (Fall 1980).

Greenwood, Michael. "Research on Internal Migration in the United States: A Survey." *Journal of Economic Literature* 13, no. 2 (1975).

Grotz, Reinhold. *Entwicklung, Struktur und Dynamik der Industrie im Wirtschaftsraum Stuttgart.* Stuttgart: Geographische Institute, University of Stuttgart, 1971.

Gunn, Peter. *A Concise History of Italy.* London: Thames & Hudson, 1971.

Habakkuk, Hrothgar J. *American and British Technology in the Nineteenth Century.* Cambridge: Cambridge University Press, 1962.

Haber, L. F. *The Chemical Industry during the Nineteenth Century.* Oxford: Clarendon Press, 1958.

————. *The Chemical Industry 1900–1930.* Oxford: Clarendon Press, 1971.

Henderson, William Otto. *Industrial Britain under the Regency 1814–18.* London: Frank Cass & Co., 1968.

Hoffmann-Nowotny, Hans-Joachim. "Global Social Aspects of Relationships between Trade Unions and Migrant Workers." *Migration Today* (1968).

Holborn, Hajo. *A History of Modern Germany 1840–1945.* New York: Knopf, 1969.

Holt, Alix. *Alexandra Kollontai, Selected Writings.* Westport, Conn.: Lawrence Hill & Co., 1977.

Horowitz, Daniel L. *The Italian Labor Movement.* Cambridge: Harvard University Press, 1963.

Hunecke, Volker. *Arbeiterschaft und Industrielle Revolution in Mailand 1859–1892.* Göttingen, FRG: Vandenhoek & Ruprecht, 1978.

Hunt, James C. *The People's Party in Württemberg and Southern Germany 1890–1914.* Stuttgart: E. Klett, 1975.

————. "The Egalitarianism of the Right: The Agrarian League in Southwest Germany 1893–1914." *Journal of Contemporary History* 10, no. 3 (1975).

Isaac, Julius. *Economics of Migration.* London: Kegan Paul, Trench, Trubner, & Co., 1947.

Joll, James. *Europe since 1870.* Harmondsworth, England: Penguin Books, 1973.

Kindleberger, Charles P. *Manias, Panics, and Crashes.* London: Macmillan, 1978.

Kirk, Dudley. *Europe's Population in the Interwar Years.* Geneva: League of Nations, 1946.

Klein, H. S. "The Integration of Italian Immigrants into the United States and Argentina: A Comparative Analysis." *The American Historical Review* 88, no. 2 (1983).

Krane, Ronald E. ed. *International Labor Migration in Europe.* New York: Praeger, 1979.

Landesarchivdirektion Baden-Württemberg. *Das Land Baden-Württemberg.* Stuttgart: Verlag W. Kohlhammer, 1977.

Lee, W. Robert. ed. *European Demography and Economic Growth.* London: Croom Helm, 1979.

Lenin, V. I. *Imperialism, the Highest Stage of Capitalism.* 1916. Reprint. Moscow: Progress Publishers, 1978.

McNeill, William H., and Adams, Ruth S., ed. *Human Migration, Patterns and Policies.* Bloomington: Indiana University Press, 1978.

Maschke, Erich, and Sydow, Jürgen, ed. *Zur Geschichte der Industrialisierung in den sudwestdeutschen Städten.* Mannheim: Jan Thorbecke Sigmaringen, 1977.

Moller, Herbert, ed. *Population Movements in Modern European History.* New York: Macmillan, 1964.

Moore, Wilbert E. *Economic Geography of Eastern and Southern Europe.* Geneva: League of Nations, 1945.

Näf, Werner. *Deutschland und die Schweiz.* Bern: Verlag Herbert Lang, 1936.

Nettl, John Peter. *Rosa Luxemburg*. London: Oxford University Press, 1966.

Paine, Suzanne. "Replacement of the West European migrant labour system by investment in the European periphery." In *Underdeveloped Europe,* edited by Dudley Seers, Bernard Schaffer, and Marja-Lilsa Kiljunen. Brighton, England: Harvester Press, 1979.

Palmer, R. R. *A History of the Modern World*. New York: Knopf, 1956.

Panta, Lorenzo del. "Italy." In *European Demography and Economic Growth,* edited by W. Robert Lee. London: Croom Helm, 1979.

Piore, Michael. *Birds of Passage*. Cambridge: Cambridge University Press, 1979.

Pollard, Sidney, ed. *Region and Industrialisation, Studies of the Role of the Region in the Economic History of the Last Two Centuries*. Göttingen, FRG: Vandenhoeck & Ruprecht, 1980.

———. *Peaceful Conquest, the Industrialization of Europe, 1760–1970*. Oxford: Oxford University Press, 1981.

Procacci, Giuliano. *History of the Italian People*. London: Weidenfeld & Nicolson, 1968.

Rees, Henry. *Italy, Switzerland, and Austria*. London: George Harrap & Co., 1974.

Rosoli, Gianfausto, ed. *Un secolo di emigrazione Italiana: 1876–1976*. Roma: Centro Studi Emigrazione, 1978.

Salomone, William. *Italy in the Giolittian Era*. Philadelphia: University of Pennsylvania Press, 1960.

Schadt, Jörg, and Schmierer, Wolfgang. *Die SPD in Baden-Württemberg und ihre Geschichte*. Stuttgart: Verlag W. Kohlhammer, 1979.

Schiff, E. *Industrialization without National Patents*. Princeton: Princeton University Press, 1971.

Schleimann, Jorgen. "The Life and Work of Willi Münzenberg." *Soviet Survey* (April 1965).

Schomerus, Heilwig. *Die Arbeiter der Maschinenfabrik Esslingen*. Stuttgart: Ernst Klett Verlag, 1977.

Schröder, Wilhelm H. *Arbeitergeschichte und Arbeiterbewegung*. Frankfurt: Campus Verlag, 1978.

Scoville, Warren C. *The Persecution of Huguenots and French Economic Development 1680–1720*. Berkeley: University of California Press, 1960.

Serpieri, Arrigo. *La guerra e le classi rurali italiane*. Bari, Italy: Gius Laterzo & Figli, 1930.

Serra, Enrico. "Italian Emigration to France during Crispi's First Government (1887–1891)." *Journal of European Economic History* (Spring 1978).

Tegel, Susan. "Ludwig Frank and the German Social Democrats." Ph.D. diss., London School of Economics, 1971.

Thistlethwaite, Frank. "Migration from Europe Overseas in the Nineteenth and Twentieth Centuries." In *Population Movements in Modern European History,* edited by Herbert Moller. New York: Macmillan, 1964.

Thomas, Brinley, ed. *Economics of International Migration*. London: Macmillan, 1958.

———. *Migration and Economic Growth*. Cambridge: Cambridge University Press, 1954.

————. "The Positive Contribution by Immigrants." In *U.S. Economic History, Selected Readings.* Edited by H. N. Scheiber. New York: Knopf, 1964.

Thompson, Warren S. *Population Problems.* New York: McGraw Hill, 1942.

Tilly, Louise A. "Urban Growth, Industrialization, and Women's Employment in Milan, Italy, 1881–1911." *Journal of Urban History* 3, no. 4 (1977).

Trease, Geoffrey. *The Italian Story.* London: Macmillan, 1963.

Tuchman, Barbara. *The Proud Tower.* London: Hamish Hamilton, 1962.

Walker, Mack. *Germany and the Emigration 1816–1885.* Cambridge: Harvard University Press, 1964.

Webster, Richard A. *Industrial Imperialism in Italy 1908–1915.* Berkeley: University of California Press, 1975.

White, Paul, and Woods, Robert, eds. *The Geographical Impact of Migration.* London: Longman, 1980.

Windell, George G. *The Catholics and German Unity 1866–1871.* Minneapolis: University of Minnesota Press, 1954.

Wordsworth, William. *The Prelude: Book VI.* 1805. In *The Norton Anthology of English Literature.* Vol. 2. New York: W. W. Norton & Co., 1962.

Zeller, Bernhard. *Hermann Hesse in Selbstzeugnissen und Bilddokumenten.* Reinbek bei Hamburg: Rowolt Taschenbuch Verlag, 1963.

INDEX

DATE DUE

DEC 08 99			
GAYLORD			PRINTED IN U.S.A.